THE MANAGER'S CRAFT

Exercising Control
Building Commitment
Sustaining Productivity

Glenn Bassett

Copyright © 2012 by Glenn A. Bassett

ISBN#: 978-1491055397

1. Leadership,
2. History of Human Relations in Industry,
3. Human Relations Practices,
4. Operations Management Principles.

Cover and interior design, author's photo by Artful Image - Paula Severino

Table of Contents

FORWARD

The twentieth century was an era of spectacular advance in scientific knowledge and technological invention. The largest part of that advance occurred after mid-century as growth in world population accelerated, burgeoning from 2.5 billion to just past six billion at century's end. The consequence was a cascade of social and economic innovation. The world shrank as technically advanced transportation and communications systems opened access to its furthest corners. The simplicity of small town life was invaded by electronic media and mass marketing. Mass society and global economics came to dominance. Everything became more complicated.

Of necessity, enhanced systems and methods of industrial organization were required in support of the increased complexity of organized endeavor. The new science of logistics that had organized World War II military global supply lines now migrated to industry where it would boost the efficiency of post-war motor car production. Domestic production of nuclear age energy on a base of nuclear fission went forward under a complex engineering partnership of government and industry. Exploration of outer space imposed space-age technical complexity onto the management of quality processes, safety standards, personnel selection, and financial control systems that have since become business standard. The simplicity of the corner grocery store where the manager once knew the price and stock quantity of every item is now the complexity of a modern supermarket where bar codes read an item price set last night in a distant corporate office and maintain a running inventory. Manual labor assembly of just about every product is replaced by or heavily supplemented with automation. The 1950s accountant in green eyeshade now sits in front of a computer screen to summarize and analyze financial data collected electronically from multiple distant operations.

Through this half century of accelerating change in business practices, the craft of managing people has changed little. Workers are offered the prevailing market wage that compensates time worked and are assigned pay raises based on economic and industry conditions. Promotions are based on fitness and facility performing the job as judged by the boss. Bosses periodically write and convey a formal appraisal review that will likely depress rather than raise individual productivity. Most workers can expect to work the still unchanged eight hour day, forty hour week until the still normal retirement age of 65. Unless specifically constrained by law, continued employment is at the employer's will. The interests of laborer and manager that were long divided by class distinction are still rarely reconciled, usually adversarial. Workers are urged to be more productive, bosses exhorted to be more democratic. In an economy of world class production management, the craft of managing continues to plod along at a horse and buggy pace.

That is not to suggest that the management of people resources has gone forward entirely without change. Initiated near century's turn and progressing through World War II, innovative programs of research focused on productivity in the workplace established a broad, new foundation for development of management practices. By the 1960s communities of academically based researchers were at work examining the influence of worker job satisfaction, commitment, and participation on work output. Experiments with wages, job structure, and work goals as incentives to higher productivity were designed and implemented. Super-productive organizations were identified and dissected to draw out their secrets. Business schools grew like mushrooms on academic soil, soaking up the best research knowledge and theory as mind fodder for their eager students. Economics was made the language of business, and high finance became its most profitable calling. A history of progress built on Henry Ford's moving assembly line and Frederick Taylor's stop watch work standards was updated and consolidated for application to mass production efficiency. The technology of cost effective, prioritized production advanced as the craft of management languished. Lost in a maze of fuzzy motivational theorizing and popular management ideology, the practice of management became detached from its surest point of anchorage: disciplined commitment to productive activity.

From my privileged perspective as a human resource policy analyst in one of America's great corporations, I followed the slow progress of management as an emerging craft. The opportunity to bring it all together came with a second career as management professor and business school dean in a vigorous regional institution that was navigating the troubled waters of academic change. In this setting a small management faculty covered the wide variety of courses that an accredited business program must offer. Limited faculty ruled out the kind of narrow academic specialization that is characteristic of large business school programs.

In its place there was opportunity to teach a full range of management subject matter. My course assignments ranged from operations management to interpersonal relationships, entrepreneurship to corporate strategy, labor law to personnel research, general systems theory to international business culture. A parallel, ongoing opportunity to support regional small businesses brought it together in practice. What remained was to sort through the mass of facts, ideas, methods and research to find an integrative theme that would move the craft of managing forward into new work space. The product of that sorting and assimilation is offered here.

When subjected to the test of utility, much of the central management theory and research still offered in the core of the business curriculum is more museum than practical application quality. Standard text coverage includes the lore of Henry Ford's mass production system, Frederick Taylor's "scientific management" innovations, Elton Mayo's Hawthorne study with its thrust at workplace enlightenment as well as a summary of job satisfaction, worker participation and motivational research. Most continue to be presented and interpreted within the prevailing theme of enlightened management, despite extensive and adequate demonstration that enlightenment alone has consistently failed to deliver the high productivity expected. Critical connections among the pieces must have been missed along the way.

Some of those connections were in plain sight but obscured by the enlightened workplace premise. Taylor successfully raised productivity by doggedly setting high output standards. Without ill feeling or rancor, he disciplined those workers who resisted meeting standards and paid fairly those who met them. It worked. Henry Ford built on Taylor's methods to ingeniously optimize capacity utilization of labor and machinery with the moving assembly line. By demanding productivity under threat of dis-employment he raised productivity to a level where exceptionally good blue collar pay allowed workers to buy their own motor cars. Hawthorne and other early research agendas overcame worker distrust to enlist commitment with a blend of fair pay, management support and ordinary discipline. Obsessive focus on popular ideology that permeated early research downplayed fair pay and ignored discipline as contributors to high productivity. The enthusiastically received 1947 Harwood manufacturing study concluded that worker participation could overcome worker resistance to meeting high work standards but offered no clarity about what participation was. Progress for the manager's craft was side-tracked and stalled for decades.

Interpretation of these early research projects overlooked the significance of worker commitment as the critical factor underpinning high productivity. Emphasis on good feelings, democracy, worker satisfaction and participative management offered no tangible progress in the manager's craft. Also absent in this dominantly ideological interpretation of early research was any grasp of the importance of simple discipline. By ignoring the relevance of authority and discipline the management teaching curricula left out a critical piece of the productivity equation. Like salesmen promoting an untested prototype, management professors and business consultants emphasized the glitz as they avoided mention of the less attractive or less understood features of the management process.

After a century of evolution in labor practices, it would seem that authority and discipline need not continue as a source of embarrassment or evasion. They are essential to coordinated economic effort. The practice of "leadership", as voluminously treated in print and seminar, continues to suggest that good managers can altogether avoid invoking either by simply being democratic. Regrettably, that is a false message. There are limits to acceptable behavior in every organization. When breached, those limits must be enforced. Failure to act does not preserve authority, it erodes it. Work discipline and worker commitment deserve higher rank in their contribution to the craft of managing. Those are working realities that managing must encompass. The effectiveness of good discipline and worker commitment as bases of productivity were ignored.

The structure of the book is organized to bring managerial authority and generation of worker commitment to the front as prime supports of high productivity. Part I begins by going immediately to an evaluation of multiple forms of behavioral control in the workplace. The principal managerial and workplace inducements that elicit desired work behavior are surveyed and evaluated. Control of worker behavior through use of economic incentives, training and leadership influence are examined. The limitations of conventionally taught theories of work motivation are critiqued. The power of a manager's personal influence to navigate crisis and uncertainty is examined. A compilation of solid research science is described that suggests that straightforward clarity in establishing work standards may be the most effective motivator of increased productivity. Research that describes the effectiveness of difficult goals in raising productivity is offered as the alternative to motivational theory. The manager who faces non-productive, dangerous or disruptive behavior must know how to set the boundaries of acceptable action through appropriate exercise of authority. Discipline is the indispensable last line of behavioral control that, itself, must be practiced within high discipline. The philosophy, rules and realities of applied discipline are candidly assessed. The moral and legal framework within which a manager exercises workplace control is outlined. The context of state and federal law that constrains the manager's craft is put in perspective with a review of at-will employment, wage and hour legislation, and labor relations issues.

Part II pulls together the traditional array of research on behavior at work that has become standard fare in management teaching and texts. Early "breakthroughs" in motivational thinking are examined as useful places to begin because of their obvious failings from a mix of flawed science and extravagant ideological ardor. They offer a fund of convenient, extensive and well documented workplace research from the early and mid-century eras that can be dissected and reinterpreted for lessons that were formerly glossed over, missed or ignored. This material is taught in almost all present day management courses and is familiar to many. It begins with the almost comical persistence of research in dogged pursuit of a causal linkage running from job satisfaction to productivity. The earnestness with which worker participation in management decision making has been promoted as the solution to workplace discord is examined. These shop worn hypotheses are revisited for their historical relevance as well as for the evidence they offer that worker commitment is the more certain path to attaining high productivity performance. Participation is critiqued for being less a contribution to management practice than a failure of conceptual clarity in understanding worker behavior. Job satisfaction is downgraded from centrality as a performance motivator, but kept in the manager's sights as worthy of a proper degree of control through use of straightforward measures. An understanding of how managers can moderate worker job dissatisfaction through setting constructive expectations is offered, and the utility of low cost attitude surveys in containing job dissatisfaction is described. A manager's guide to the opportunities and complexities of pay systems and incentives is presented as doorway to knowledge that may allow a manager to use pay as an incentive for improved performance despite its limitations for that purpose. To address matters of job fit, those skills and knowledge are illuminated that permit a manager to identify demonstrably relevant qualities of worker talent and temperament. The power that resides in getting to know one's workers as individuals through a purposeful conversation is explored, and paths to its mastery are appraised.

Part III launches into explication of the fundamental tools of productivity management in the operations sense. These are work specialization, productive efficiency, capacity utilization and sound judgment in setting priorities. Managerial productivity rests on recognition that although task specialization is fundamental to economic efficiency it is, regrettably, a major restraint on release of human productive potential. Much that each person has to offer is omitted from the job description. Presumption of fixed job design operates as barrier to the task redesign that is needed to keep up with the steadily advancing curve of experience. Continual redesign of jobs is crucial to accommodating the inevitability of ongoing technological and social evolution. The march of innovation and discovery makes regular, periodic job enhancements not only desirable but also essential. Managing the learning curve by introducing periodic job enhancements is appraised as a necessary base for sustenance of high productivity.

The production genius of Henry Ford and task engineering insights of Frederick Winslow Taylor are described and appraised as the foundations of both the benefits and deficiencies of modern economic systems. Those advances that were achieved continue to represent astounding milestones of industrial efficiency. Efficiency, though, is appraised as less a boon to mankind than as an economic whip that drives perpetually increased productivity regardless of social consequences. Evidence is offered in support of skepticism concerning the assumed equivalence of productivity with number of hours worked. The prevailing economic shift toward specialty production and service is examined for its implications for efficiency and capacity utilization. An exposition is offered as to how recognition and management of system constraints -

bottlenecks - has become the principal requisite for maximizing labor and equipment capacity usage in short run production and service offerings. The challenges that come with managing risk, upholding standards, protecting the business' good name and assuring safety are assessed against demands for perpetual pursuit of profit and performance priorities.

Broader, more nuanced interpretation of available evidence provides the foundation of conclusions and recommendations offered here. A solid empirical underpinning is central to justification of the case that a superior approach to the manager's craft exists. Research must be clearly examined and reevaluated if a general reformulation of long standard management theory is to be achieved. Throughout the book the research studies cited and technical operating methodologies employed are presented in the simplest possible terms without any major sacrifice of clarity and precision. The methods of science that have informed this synthesis of theory and practice are stripped of jargon to make them accessible to every reader.

Prevailing management ideology is challenged and rebuilt on a base of sound logic and good science that includes the key elements of operations research methodology. Inclusion of the operations dimension of management is by necessity. The technology of operations research based production methods must be clearly understood and applied if the craft of managing is to move forward. To achieve clarity the core of industrial operations technology and theory is translated into non-technical terms so it can be installed in the manager's tool box. Its lack is a critical limitation on productivity that could override everything else.

The manager's craft is a set of tools, ideas, and principles drawn from science, theory and experience that are custom blended to fit the situation. The mix of the pattern will change from time to time, circumstance to circumstance. Exercising control, building commitment and sustaining productivity are the superstructure on which each pattern will be hung. From all the ways that control and authority can be applied, the most effective will be formed. From an understanding of all the forms that commitment can take, the surest approach to nurturing it will emerge. Joined through the manager's skill, control and commitment will sustain high productivity.

With a little luck, this will be a fun read and a solid career enhancer too.

PART I:

CONTROL AND THE EXERCISE OF AUTHORITY

1. THE FOUNDATIONS OF CONTROL AND AUTHORITY

Control of behavior in an organizational setting depends on the existence of accepted formal authority. The right to hire, fire and discipline stands behind every instruction or rule set forth by the bosses. Authority in use, though, remains the most misapprehended, misused and costly resource among all those employed to direct work behavior. More careers are stalled, more anger and confusion is generated, more time is wasted through the inept use of authority than from any other source. A personal need to possess and exercise authority distracts and confuses the manager who fears appearing weak or lacking resolve in its use. Fear of retributive blow-back paralyzes action where avoidance of error and blame grips that resolve. Yet, without authority in the background of manager-worker relationship, not much will be accomplished by a team brought together through little more than economic self-interest. Authority is the fundamental lever of control in the pursuit of business goals and objectives. Its gets the job done.

Skillful use of authority arises from opportunity for practice. Few business organizations offer training in how to use authority. Military and civil police organizations are notable exceptions. Soldiers are sensitized to its use through training under severe authority. The schooling of military officers subjects candidates to something that is near excess in exercise of authority, first as the butt of brutal treatment, later as the agents of it. Where that training is effective, military leaders learn how to measure the extent of authority that is appropriate to the situation. They know what harsh authority feels like and where to draw the line in its application. They also know that the secret of successful control thorough authority is measuring disciplinary action so that it is just sufficient to the circumstances.

A useful analogy is offered by the challenge of maintaining control when driving a vehicle at high speed. The inexperienced driver lacks sensitivity to the hurtling mass of steel unleashed by an accelerator pedal. A rough or slippery road, the sudden appearance of a hazard, an unexpected mechanical failure demands exactly the right degree of response in steering and braking. The exhilaration of new power can cloud judgment of risk. The wrong move will sacrifice control to the laws of physics. Experiments with powered vehicular momentum daily breach the limits of control on the highways producing hard won experience that may or may not be survived.

Developing skill at control of the busy, ongoing workplace is little different from acquiring the ability to accurately drive a golf ball, shoot a ball through the basketball hoop or pound a nail. It takes practice. For ultimate success each also requires the right tools and knowledge of the processes. To avoid costly trial and error one must first discover what works and what does not. The newly appointed supervisor or manager of a work unit is put in the same position as every new auto driver, golfer, athlete or carpenter. With little more than experience as a subject of authority, he/she must apply it as an experiment in gaining and exercising control. If there is too much self-possession in its use or too little confidence in one's judgment of the situation there can be painful consequences. Hard won experience will, at best, be the minimum product of that pain.

The source of all legitimate social authority is civil law and custom, created over an extended history of human social struggle. The foundations of both are the natural human resources of physical strength, maturity, skill and knowledge. In a variety of blends, these resources continue to shape the universal competition for social dominance as it is moderated and refereed by present day law and custom.

The necessary instruments of management control include economic incentives, personal influence, training that instills good habits, and, where necessary, coercive action in the form of discipline. We begin with a brief survey of these four tools and the variety of forms they take along with the problems they can create. As we move into future chapters, their use will be more fully developed.

INCENTIVES

Incentives begin with pay and benefits. They expand to include opportunity for advancement in pay and status, for acquisition of new or advanced skills, for provision of desirable working conditions, sometimes even for a preferred and convenient work schedule. Incentives have potentially significant cost and can require trade-offs to reconcile conflict inherent among options. Undesirable working conditions might be offset by higher pay or a better work schedule. Pleasant working conditions might allow for a less desirable work schedule. Lower pay is often appropriate to account for the costs of low productivity while a work skill is being developed. Because pay and benefits are typically administered through a one-size-fits-all package, their use as incentive is limited. Within the constraints of uniform company systems of pay and benefits, the pragmatic manager may still find opportunity to effectively use other incentives like scheduling, skill acquisition and promotional opportunity.

The incentive value of pay and benefits could be improved if prevailing systems were more flexible than those in current use. The most commonly employed compensation policy is to pay the market rate for the applicable skill or experience and adjust periodically to reflect increased "cost of living". Most such increases are, at best, minuscule and incremental. Pay adjustments of any amount typically require multiple levels of approval. This puts a brake on increases that might offer real incentive. Substantial increase adjustments are approved only where they are obviously merited by demonstrated productivity, or where there is concern that the exceptional productive capability will be lost to competitors.

Standard compensation policy thus assures control of base wage costs and contributes minimally to worker commitment and productivity. Payment at market rate typically means paying the average of the market without consideration for the range of minimum to maximum. Often the tendency is to pursue competitive cost advantage by paying newly hired employees well below market average. That will disappoint those new workers who expect better pay. Low pay accepted through necessity is a hidden, deferred issue of inequity. Pay level expectations of job candidates are rarely known or accounted for and the applicant's need for employment will likely trump hopes for higher pay. The result of perceived inadequacy of pay can be diminished work commitment and productivity. On any terms, starting pay rates seldom offer much incentive beyond coming to work regularly. At the outset of an employment relationship, rigid wage cost policies can thus become a concealed barrier to worker commitment and productivity.

Benefits like medical, life and disability insurances originally came into being when it was recognized that maintaining a stable, healthy, undistracted work force was important as foundation for building worker commitment and productivity. Sheltered from taxation under the Federal income tax code, benefits became a relatively cost effective way to support those objectives. The incentive value of benefits to employees, though, is often questionable. Workers have widely disparate needs for the benefits offered. A worker's age and family status play a large role in the importance of retirement and health benefits. Young, unmarried individuals find limited value in those benefits, and, when asked, often express a preference to take their cash value in direct pay. Employees married with families are likely to want employment with good health insurance. Older workers are more concerned about retirement. Working parents may need flexible scheduling and more paid time off for family requirements. One size does not satisfactorily fit all when standardized benefit packages are offered. For purposes of cost control and convenience of administration, though, a uniform benefits package is adopted by most employers.

The result is a compromise designed to fit the "average worker" who is likely to be a statistical fiction.

The standard package of benefits, thus, may or may not contribute to worker commitment and productivity. Doubt should be entertained when assessing whether most benefits can, in fact, even offer any performance incentive at all. Retirement benefits that have not vested (the worker does not yet own the benefit), along with progressively lengthened vacation time, may create an obstacle to changing jobs when there is obvious benefit in doing so. The commitment to remaining employed created by those obstacles may or may not be beneficial to the employer depending on market factors and the quality of the worker's job performance.

Insurance against sickness of worker or family members was once thought to free wage earners from worry about medical bills and allow them to focus on work performance. As health benefits have become prevalent they have come to be expected as a standard element of the benefits package. The lack of health insurance then becomes a disappointment that may diminish commitment because its existence is expected. The one clear incentive that health coverage has created is for workers to ignore the real cost of medical care. Thus, high demand for health services and lack of concern for cost has driven the cost of health coverage to ever higher levels. Medical insurance has become a trap for employers. It can be a source of contention rather than an incentive to productivity.

The limitation of benefits plans as incentives has not been entirely overlooked. In the decade of the 1980s social science research illuminated the lack of incentive value that was being bought with expensive worker benefits. It was asked if increased value might be obtained from benefits where employees chose "cafeteria" style from a menu of available benefits. Workers, for instance, might elect to trade off some part of retirement savings or elements of medical coverage for increased direct pay or additional paid time off. Or, they might opt for added retirement benefits over longer vacations. Introducing choice in the packaging of one's employment benefits, the reasoning went, might be a way to increase the incentive value of benefits. In practice offering such choice can create problems. The greater the opportunity extended to a worker for working out the incentive package, the greater the amount of management time and skill that must be applied to negotiating its shape. Lack of uniformity in worker incentive packages invites confusion and yet more negotiation. The down-side of flexibly packaged benefits is that it opens the door to haggling over benefits. This introduces new complications into the employment relationship. It also begs questions about their tax exempt status. The original level of interest in cafeteria benefits schemes quickly diminished when these constraints became apparent. Some interest persists, but, on the whole, the potential for incentive power from cafeteria styled benefits continues to languish.

Cookie-cutter incentive packages like market based pay and fixed incentive packages introduce rigidity that robs them of the incentive power that could be obtained from flexible design. Until significant commitment and productivity increases are obtained from them, pay and benefits packages will continue to tend toward uniformity, both within organizations and across industries. They have become part of the dilemma that characterizes work incentives in general. The acquisition of the needed management experience to apply flexible incentives is risky and costly. Because it is not practiced and developed by working managers the opportunity for increased control, commitment and productivity in their application is lost. Despite adjustments that have been made in the tax code to accommodate limited cafeteria benefits plans, real flexibility continues to be elusive. More imagination is needed.

As a source of control over worker behavior on the job, incentives like pay and benefits are very crude levers. They are insufficient in themselves to elicit anything more than adequate work performance. The current potential for improving that leverage rests mostly with increasing the skill and experience of the individual working manager. Approached pragmatically one employee at a time, improvement may be obtained. Until supplemented with effective work motivation founded on commitment and sound operations methods, incentives offer only the base line from which to build toward commitment.

INFLUENCE

That part of control which is beyond incentives and without habit or coercion is what can usefully be termed influence. The holy grail of management control is any form of direct influence upon the worker that, alone, increases commitment and productivity. Influence, where it is produced, is largely or wholly without direct monetary cost. In its purest form, it takes the form of effective leadership. Influence as most people understand it is the encouragement of commitment and increased productivity without resort to threats or incentives. Just how that comes about, though, is not always easy to nail down in useful specifics. It is likely to be a function of circumstances.

Much leadership influence is the product of habit and custom. The cloak of custom-based authority found in uniforms and other formal dress has clear and consistent effect on behavior. Titles like dad, mom, teacher, pastor, can in themselves produce influence over actions of others by those who own them. Most of the boss's influence, though, is from tangible control of work behavior through incentives and threat of their loss. Leadership goes beyond these direct forces of control to elicit genuinely voluntary and unforced response. The test of real influence is the absence of incentives and threats. It arises out a leader's capacity to elicit from others commitment to and shared focus on results through force of personality alone.

Crisis often creates circumstances favorable to influence. Much spontaneous need and readiness for leadership is the consequence of shared threat or confusion. Organization of response to the September 11, 2001 terrorist destruction of New York's World Trade Center towers arose out of just that kind of threat and confusion. The mayor of New York, Rudi Giuliani, was the focus of custom-based expectations for leadership. Close to the scene in his Manhattan City Hall office he immediately took formal command of the situation. First responders and others faced with the requirement of leadership action reacted within a framework of prior planning and training under the mayor's official leadership. Their influence relied on formal roles and social custom. Most such leadership is ceremonial. But in one domain, leadership in the face of the 9/11 disaster literally emerged out of the dust and disorder solely on the basis of influence.

Following the collapse of the twin towers, the job of clearing the incredible mound of wreckage and rubble was taken over by a pair of municipal bureaucrats through little more than the exercise of their influence. The commissioner of the New York City Department of Design and Construction and his operations director assumed control of the clean-up without being asked or told to do so. Indeed, prior to 9/11 the DDC was never even included in drafts of the city's plans for emergency response to disaster.[1]

The commissioner of DDC, Kenneth Holden, was a career bureaucrat, his lieutenant, Michael Burton, an engineer. Between them they had the political know-how, heavy construction industry contacts and the technical knowledge needed to coordinate the task. No one told them they were in charge. They were assigned no formal authority. They were on the scene, they knew what had to be done and they assumed leadership. Indeed, they moved in so quickly and competently that those appropriate Federal and State agencies which might have been involved never needed to mobilize.

Holden and Burton immediately called to the scene those large contractors who could marshal the necessary skill and equipment to begin attacking the rubble in support of search for survivors and bodies. No contracts were negotiated, no bids requested. Firms they knew from experience as equal to the task were told to start clearing and aiding in the recovery search for survivors and bodies.

The work was divided among four contractors so that each was assigned a physical segment of the total job. Holden and Burton coordinated contractors' efforts with the police and firemen who doggedly and passionately labored to find their own missing brothers and civilian dead. They made decisions as trivial as solving turf disputes between agencies and as critical as how to prevent collapse of walls that held back river water from surging into the city's underground transport systems. Possessing, though never formally assigned authority to make such critical decisions, they presided over daily operating conferences where priorities were set and operating differences were settled. With no formal authority or charter, they effectively directed the monumental task of "unbuilding" the World Trade Center. Relying on influence alone they exercised control over this crisis situation.

Indeed, leadership capability is often associated with just such crisis situations. Crisis inflicts uncertainty on all involved, with the risk of still greater crisis arising if it is not met competently. Crisis demands and tests leadership. Those caught in this chaos and feeling its distress are especially open to influence and amenable to control of those who offer leadership influence. The leader who rises to the challenge and organizes response to it can exercise influence. His/her reputation as a leader may approach an heroic mode in the process.

Extraordinary opportunities for discovery or achievement can be magnets for aspiring leaders. Almost any situation that generates high interest, excitement or anticipation calls for and creates leaders who channel and focus the actions of those who must respond. War is guaranteed to create heroes out of ordinary politicians and soldiers. Contests of every kind generate the need for leaders. Coaches of competitive sports often enjoy exceptional leadership status because of the emotion invested by team members and their fans in the competition to win. Coaches thereby exercise an exceptional degree of control over team members' performances and may wield social influence well beyond the boundaries of the team and sport. The title Coach is itself invested with considerable social significance. Coaches of local teams are often also local heroes.

Candidates for political office depend on influence to a great extent, perhaps to the utmost, in generating voter support. Every election represents some level of crisis of political stability. Incentives in the form of political promises play a part in securing votes but political promises can cut both ways. The currency of politics is influence in the form of rhetoric which appeals to voters' sense of a political crisis. Passionate speaches, fervent warnings against the harmfulness of an opponent's policies and positions, calls to faith in ideology, all generate influence that sway elections in huge measure. This is control through influence that approaches its purest form.

Response to the influence of a leader arises out of the anxiety of those who are faced with crisis circumstances or exciting opportunities. When there are no clear incentives to action and no habits of training set in place, emotional intensity takes over seeking help and guidance. Indeed, almost any form of uncertainty, confusion or striving can open the door to exercise of influence. The working manager who is sensitive to situational need for leadership can discover those intense situations that have potential for exercise of influence.

TRAINING

Training is the blunt instrument of control. It is effective in establishing response to fully anticipated situations, costly to implement and inflexible in the face of surprise. Training requires either controlled structure that simulates actual performance, or long-term practice across time that establishes the appropriate and needed work behavior. Both can be costly. Simulation can require a large up-front investment in machinery and processes while direct experience must allow for mistakes and accidents. The costs of the former are immediate, those of the latter, deferred. Expecting mistakes and accidents to be avoided or minimal is enough to tilt the preference toward training through practical experience. Simulation tends to be reserved for those performances that are exceptionally hazardous or potentially deadly. Training astronauts and airline pilots, for instance, justifies use of costly computerized simulation equipment.

The more common approach to job training is to put the learner to work at the task under the watch of an experienced coach or mentor. Most young people learn to drive an automobile in this fashion. The trainer rides with the novice driver offering cautions and pointers. The driver masters the basics of automobile control using the steering wheel, accelerator and brakes. A feel for how the vehicle handles is established. Few trainers go beyond the basics, leaving the new driver to obtain his/her own experience with performance of the vehicle when it is operated near its limits of speed and stability. Trainers hope that nothing bad will occur when those tests come. Something frequently does. The odds favor mistakes and accidents. Because the cost of training through experience defers the costs of failure, those costs tend to be underestimated. They can nonetheless be substantial.

In many instances, the need for simulated experience can be addressed by blending training through practice with ad hoc simulations of the potentially more critical events, especially those that involve response to high risk and difficult performance. A great proportion of fatal car accidents arise out of the attempt to control the car the way one would control a bicycle. There is no beginning appreciation of the physics of control under high speed momentum among new drivers. The result is over-control that loses all control. A novice driver needs to learn the feel of stopping suddenly at high speed, or of how to maintain control on a slippery road. The new driver must practice handling those emergency response situations where control of the vehicle can be lost. The astute mentor takes advantage of opportunity to simulate emergency stops on slippery roadways or in an empty mall parking lot on a snowy day.

Much of a manager's training through direct experience involves learning to control the performance of workers with verbal commands. Rarely is there adequate appreciation of the weakness of words for shaping job performance. Even where ordinary words are the stuff of instruction, there can be confusion in their application. Where the language of work involves technical terminology that must first be learned, the level of difficulty is still greater. The manager who controls with communication must self-monitor the process to identify emergent failure when coaching with even simple, clear instructions. The test of effective control through words will come later when critical control must be achieved under difficult, stressful circumstances. At the core of the training process, there will always be an interplay of training between the controller and the controlled that requires clarity, consistency and tests of the limits. Here the manager will be trained along with the trainee.

Incidental actions can become trained cues in themselves. Clearing one's throat with a cough, looking at the floor with a slight frown, standing with arms stiffly crossed may occasionally precede the manager's criticism. Workers cue on subtle behaviors that their boss may inadvertently offer. Upon presentation of those cues they may become distracted and unproductive or even flee the situation that has been associated with past criticism. Controlling with words always includes gestures and postures whether they are intended or not. Managers must train themselves to be aware of their words and actions if they are to be effective in shaping a worker's behavior.

COERCION

Direct, harsh orders, formal disciplinary action and separation from employment are the last line of control. Much of the time they are admission that control has been lost and there may be no way to recover it. Corrective action taken by the inexperienced is likely to be too late and too hasty, making matters worse. Coercive action by an inexperienced manager can easily become the equivalent of over-controlling the vehicle into an accident. Unfortunately, damage to the boss and institution are almost always hidden and deferred. Because the immediate injury is to the subordinate worker, there is likely to be little or limited learning on the manager's part. Poorly conceived disciplinary action will not be recognized as the failure of control that it could be.

Holding sway over the economic fate of another person is an awesome responsibility. The boss who is uncomfortable, or worse, too comfortable when exercising disciplinary power, risks serious damage to commitment and productivity throughout the organization. Competently wielded disciplinary authority must be fully divorced from ego issues. The manager who becomes personally and emotionally involved in the exercise of coercive power will not exercise authority well.

Discipline most always be appropriate to circumstances. Disciplinary power and authority must be used only on that rare occasion when the boundaries of proper work behavior have been clearly breached. As in the prosecution of criminal behavior under civil law there must always be solid justification on evidence of the offender's intent to commit the breach. Ignorant or inadvertent violation of the rules merits measured response that corrects the problem, not full scale punishment. Harsh discipline in the absence of willful intent will be understood as unjust or arrogant by subordinates. It is, indeed, often better to overlook an occasional inadvertent bending of the standards than to discipline harshly and hastily on limited evidence.

Discipline that affects loss of pay or separation from employment must be applied with the greatest caution and care. When there is any doubt about extent of or intent in breach of the rules, the decision to act should turn on whether there is real need to reestablish the boundaries of proper behavior for the larger organization. Unless action can be contained at the strictly personal and confidential level, discipline should always be approached as a major social event that could set off widespread social disruption in response.

The safest rule with application of all discipline, indeed, is that the need for action should be clear to everyone and the absolute minimum penalty required to make the manager's point should be applied. Simple, muted verbal warnings can be the most effective action. The best possible discipline may be an almost subtle comment like "It would be best that you not do that again." Workers respect bosses who quietly enforce the boundaries of acceptable behavior without threat or anger. Discipline that exceeds the force needed to merely restore stability will further destabilize and disrupt. While "you're fired" may be acceptable on a dramatic TV reality show, it is never the right approach in the real work place. Formal organizational discipline is the social equivalent of the hurtling momentum of a speeding automobile. Foolhardy tests of full throttle authority can do great damage. A fuller examination of how such catastrophe can be avoided will come in a later chapter on disciplinary due process.

Once invested with authority over workers and experienced in its application, a manager should rarely need to use it. If influence, incentives and training are skillfully used the mere possession of authority should confer power enough to maintain control over worker behavior. Though pay and benefits may offer little potential for control, an alert manager will look for those remaining incentives that offer opportunity for flexible application if they are to contribute to commitment and productivity. There must be sensitivity to emergence of any opportunity produced by stress or excitement where influence can be put to the service of increased commitment and productivity. Training that is appropriate will be developed to support reliable productivity under stable working conditions. Authority will be exercised only when well defined boundaries of proper action have been breached and there is little other choice. An appreciation of these resources and their limitations is the beginning of effective managerial control.

A manager's tool kit of control levers requires practice and experience in their use. Effective control begins with knowing the limitations of one's tools. The most important form of managerial control is self-control that assesses the needs and opportunities inherent in the situation. Reacting hastily and inappropriately in the face of confused or uncertain events risks major loss of control. The levers and measures that permit the manager's use of control in service of increased commitment and productivity are the subject of following chapters.

2. GOALS: MOTIVATION THEORY THAT WORKS

Direct control can be harsh and unpleasant to contemplate. In nineteenth century factories and mines control was often achieved by providing laborers with no more than a bare subsistence wage. Unwillingness to work could result in discipline that was the equivalent of a sentence to starvation. As recently as the 1930s and 1940s factory discipline in Soviet Russia extended to denial of all rights to food and shelter. Workers subject to that kind of discipline have no control of their own existence and cannot make independent choices. They do the minimum required to survive.

Civility demands better. Control must be humane. A common beginning in the pursuit of that object is to puzzle over what motivates human behavior. Seeking out the inner motives of action bypasses the ethical concerns that go with imposing direct control over the target individual's behavior. Identifying the worker's motivations is a search for the concealed control buttons that overcome the need for overt constraint.

The surest motive to action on the part of any organism is physical need. Hunger is the principal source of control for purposes of laboratory experiments with animals. Food deprivation sufficiently activates the organism so that behavior can be cleverly controlled in rats and pigeons. Theorizing about human motivation usually begins by assuming actors are well fed and comfortable, but that they have higher order needs that can be manipulated to focus behavior. The question might be posed in terms of what is it, after physiological needs like food and oxygen are met, that will motivate workers to produce. Abraham Maslow's 1943 articulation of a human need hierarchy continues to be the answer to that question for many social scientists, management writers and managers. Just how his answer contributes to control processes in the workplace has never been made fully clear. Indeed, while it can illuminate the range of natural forces that may drive action, need based motivational theory in general as well as need theory in particular has offered no practical means through which to control behavior. It has produced little beyond engaging rhetoric.[1]

Examples of contradiction in the functioning of hierarchically stacked needs as motives are easy to find. The standard Maslowian hierarchy proceeds upward from the physiological through security to affection, on to self-esteem and culminates in the abstract loftiness of self-actualization. At the most basic level of physical well being, the willingness of young women to risk starvation maintaining a radically slim body devastates the notion of food as an absolute foundation need. The readiness of spelunkers, sky divers or explosive experts to risk their lives in their spine-tingling pursuits calls to question the power of security needs in constraining risky action. Yearnings for independence of life style frequently lead to abandonment of a secure place in social and economic affairs to find one's life's calling. If such yearnings be self-actualization, that may have be defined as a fundamental need in its own right.

Actual expression of need often denies the notion of building through a hierarchy. At any level, domination of need out of its hierarchical order may erupt. Despite such criticisms similar need hierarchies continue to appear in the literature of psychology and management, freshly revised and updated. One recently proposed extension of need theory offers up sixteen basic desires that "motivate our actions and define our personalities."[2] Included among these needs are such desires as curiosity, idealism, honor, tranquility and vengeance. An even more current version updates the dimension of self-actualization by defining it as mating and parenting.[3] Needs theories of motivation are popular and make for lively discussion but they do little to address the issue of behavioral control.

The association of basic needs with personality typology introduces the possibility that motivation may be a matter of personality type rather than of levels or factors. This is not any kind of hierarchal motivation. It is smorgasbord styled motivation where any one or more idiosyncratic personal behavior strategies may become operative depending on the experience and temperament of the individual. Motivation is rendered individually specific by most popular personality typologies. Individual pattern of temperament may, indeed be the key to motivation. Dimensions of temperament developed by social scientists in recent decades have been shown useful in predicting job success. The temperamentally conscientious worker, for instance, is typically a more committed, productive worker. Calling such conscientiousness a motive, though, adds nothing to the capacity for commitment that it suggests. This issue will later be delved in more depth.

In its most operationalized iteration as proposed by Harvard psychologist David McClelland, human motivation arises out of a triad of culturally shaped personality based value factors that function like needs. In McClelland's motivation scheme, the extent of striving for achievement, or for affiliation or for power, establishes a dominant social force in the political and economic culture. McClelland proposes that the relative influence of each can be measured for individuals with sophisticated psychological projective techniques, as well as for whole societies through analysis of popular literature. The relative dominance of each can be seen in a culture's literary themes. One appeal of the McClelland approach is its applicability to economic, historical and sociological analysis of national culture. This is motivation as applied economics and politics. Its use at the individual level becomes a kind of psychoanalytic exercise.[4] Achievement is, indeed, a distinctive characteristic of committed workers that may be expressed through personal narratives. Motivation to achieve is a quality to be valued and looked for, whether it is a motive or a personality trait.

In its other various incarnations motivational speculation suffers from defects similar to those of need theory. Notions of intrinsic vs. extrinsic motivation are little more than recognition of the differences in direct and indirect control. Frederick

Hertzberg's "Two-Factor Theory" puts motivational forces like challenging work or recognition, presumed to produce satisfaction, in opposition to "hygienic" ones like pay and social status that are expected to forestall emergence of job dissatisfaction.[5] Beyond the obviously metaphorical superficiality of this approach, the problems of linking motivation to satisfaction and dissatisfaction are substantial. These become issues of rhetoric, not influence or control.

Other than food and comfort, the list of natural forces that might drive action is more an inventory of human behavioral possibilities than a specification of motives to action. Self-reports of reasons for working, working hard, or seeking work seldom offer useful information for controlling work behavior. Rather, it alerts management to the wide variety of specific motives that can inspire increased work output. The conclusion would seem to be that every individual worker must be approached as a unique bundle of needs and motives that must be specifically addressed, person by person. There is certain merit in approaching management as a search for those individual motives that create commitment and drive productivity from each worker. That is an argument that will later be rejoined. On a general level, any efficiencies that permit the working manager to directly motivate worker productivity must not be overlooked. Indeed, there is at least one demonstrated common sense answer. The most direct approach to worker motivation is simple: set clear, difficult work goals for each employee and provide real-time achievement feedback. That has long been what experienced managers do.

CLEARLY SET WORK GOALS AS MOTIVATORS

The beginnings of systematic management in pursuit of high productivity are conventionally credited to the early twentieth century work of Frederick W. Taylor. Taylor was a self-taught industrial engineer and productivity crusader. He held that there was one best method for the performance of every job and that, through rigorous implementation of his top-down, imposed work methods, every worker could achieve high production goals. Taylor almost single handedly launched the age of industrial efficiency and created the career path of industrial engineering. In factories around the world, his time and motion studies of production tasks are central to engineered efficiency and productivity.

Taylor's approach to managing, for high productivity included several revolutions in management that have since become central to industrial engineering and operations management practice. He developed detailed cost accounts for each specific product line, implemented piece-work pay systems that directly rewarded high productivity, and used stop watch time studies of tasks to establish standards for their performance. His top-down imposed measures allowed work flow to be managed for controlled, overall maximum efficiency.[6]

Labor unions and workers of the time vilified "Taylorism" as the worst form of sweat-shop management. Unionized industry that applied Taylor's Scientific Management system were then and are still sometimes characterized by intense conflict between union leaders and industrial engineers. Sadly, work stoppages and strikes in response to engineered work standards often offsets the gains of engineered efficiencies. Better answers were sought that would preserve labor peace and secure commitment to high standards of productivity. Management by Objectives, MBO, promoted by management consultant Peter Drucker, offered an alternative to Taylor's methods that held promise for improving on them.

With the 1955 publication of his book, "The Practice of Management" self-taught Austrian Management Psychologist Peter Drucker successfully parlayed a war time consulting assignment with General Motors into national status as the inventor of and authority on Management by Objectives.[7] The object of MBO was to increase employee commitment and productivity by participatively involving workers in setting goals for their work output. Drucker was convinced that involvement in the goal setting process was the key to motivating increased productivity. He believed that, while lucidness of communication and goal clarity were important supports to goal setting, and linking worker goals to organization objectives may be critical, active worker participation was indispensable to high productivity. Drucker touted worker participation as the ultimate productivity tool.

MBO was widely implemented in many US corporations and government operations. Improvements in productivity up to as much as 50% were claimed. Results were variable depending on the intensity of involvement of top management in setting goals. MBO worked best when the process became part of the business culture and was closely tied to business strategy. They were limited when there was an absence of involvement by top management in its implementation. MBO was not something that an individual working manager could adopt on his/her own initiative. Primary working level emphasis was on how to keep workers happy and thereby, productive and participative.

Management that created worker satisfaction through participation received new stress at the operating level in the age of MBO. Post war productivity research concentrated almost obsessively on worker participation and job satisfaction. Managers and psychologists focused on worker participation in decision making and satisfaction in their work as the most likely levers of productivity improvement. Scores of published research papers pursued the link between satisfaction, participation and productivity. Seminars in participative management were offered throughout industry, and an army of eager consultants carried the message of productivity through participation and worker satisfaction. Researchers earnestly sought evidence linking participation and job satisfaction with high productivity. Results were sometimes slightly positive, sometimes slightly negative, and almost always inconclusive. Something was missing.

Management Psychologist Edwin A Locke at the University of Maryland, who had long pursued a scholarly interest in Frederick

Taylor's management methods, was a leading commentator on the limitations of worker satisfaction research.[8] In his estimate Taylor's proven approach offered answers that were being overlooked. Taylor had set clear production goals, measured their achievement and provided full performance feedback to workers. Taylorism, despite its vocal detractors, had long worked to raise productivity. Ed Locke looked past worker satisfaction and participation to emphasize explicit, challenging work goals as the essential core of work motivation. In the mid 1960s, he began to focus his personal research on goal setting and performance feedback as the primary facilitators of work productivity. Locke became a prolific publisher on the subject and through his personal commitment to the issue became the hub of a community of researchers focused on goal setting as the most effective way to achieve increased productivity. In 1981, the research product of this emerging community was summarized in a major review article in the prestigious American Psychological Association journal, Psychological Review. The culmination of the goal setting research community's work was later published in 1990 as a hard cover treatise on motivational theory under the title A Theory of Goal Setting and Task Performance.[9] The motivational principles offered by goal setting research represent the most significant advances in motivational theory offered since mid-century.

THE GOAL SETTING HYPOTHESIS

Goal setting as productivity motivation is founded on a very large body of empirical research and evidence. Frederick Taylor had already demonstrated persuasively that imposed production goals could increase productivity. The difficulty with his compelled goals was that under a variety of conditions workers would actively resist their imposition. Control of work performance that relies on imposed top-down discipline, as Taylor's did, immediately raises the likelihood of push-back. Ed Locke and his community of research scholars describe how standard wage incentives combined with the manager's influence and encouragement will achieve high productivity without that push-back. Goal setting research makes clear that, although there is no simple start-button that guarantees motivation of productivity, there are skills and principles that can be mastered by the working manager to raise productivity. These skills and principles are all part of the manager's art of control. The fund of research they emerge from describes their use.

Many hundreds of goal setting research studies have been carried out with a variety of tasks. Laboratory investigations have employed puzzles, games, computational problems, card sorting, color discrimination, anagrams, prose learning, parts assembly and similar tasks that can be readily observed and measured. Field studies and simulated field studies have used paid jobs like copy typing, data entry and verification, sales performance, academic grades, the output of logging crews, freight handling, machine repair, die casting, supervising, as well as the performance of engineers on technical tasks. With scientific consistency these studies were rigorously designed with control groups, randomized assignment and other standard research techniques in place. The number and variety of these studies provides wide variation in the difficulty of tasks, the level of difficulty of goals set, the complexity of goals and problems with conflicting goals. From this fund of measured, observed task performance, the conditions under which goal setting is expected to succeed were identified and summarized.[10]

It was demonstrated that only difficult, specific goals are effective for increasing production. Do-your-best and try harder instructions produced little or no change in level of output. Compared to prior performance with "do-your-best" instructions, specification of difficult goals raised work output in ninety (90%) percent of 110 studies examined by Locke et al in their 1981 Psychological Bulletin summary of goal setting research. [11] The phenomenon was so robust and ubiquitous that those instances in which setting specific, difficult goals did not work seemed curiously uncharacteristic. For researchers, managers and supervisors involved it was sometimes surprising to observe the ease with which research subjects and workers accepted and worked toward difficult goals set for them. As a member of the original research community, this writer's first acquaintance with the phenomena came close-up in a pretest of the method with temporary workers hired to perform a simulated clerical task with specific, difficult performance goals. Activity was closely observed with the expectation of resistance or other outward sign of hard labor. There was none. It was as if there was nothing either unusual or stressful about the instruction to strive toward high output goals. Interviews of workers after completion of the task mostly solicited something like "I just tried to reach the goals you gave me." Clearly, the setting of the task and the goals themselves were enough to focus effort. Something more, though, may be needed before specific, difficult goals can become consistent over time as effective motivators.

When used with ongoing work to raise output performance over a span of time, workers must have knowledge of their performance results - feedback - so they know how they are doing. They must be able to track their performance. In the absence of tracking data, performance improvement will not occur. Difficult, specific goals and discernible feedback are required as conditions for improved productivity through goal setting. Difficult goals and performance feedback are, indeed, indispensable to managerial control of productivity in the work setting.

Even though it does work the vast proportion of time, goal setting is not uniformly effective. Goal planning failed one time in ten in the summarized research studies summarized. Clearly, other conditions can affect the level of performance that can account for those occasions when it does not work. There are, indeed, some conditions to the social setting that must be met for goal setting to work. Where goals are set at a level of difficulty that seriously challenges or prevents full achievement, it is critical that there be no fear of penalty for falling short in performance. The object must be to raise productivity to a sustainable level, not to hit every target every time. Goal setting also assumes that workers are selected, trained and skilled sufficiently to carry out all the tasks required of their work. Selection and training that properly qualifies workers to perform technical tasks is fundamental. Sometimes difficult goals may require acquisition of new or expanded skill. This can succeed so long as the worker is supported in working through to attainment of the required skill. It is expected that the pursuit of difficult goals should require marshaling of skill and effort appropriate to the level of difficulty that requires added experience and skill. Response to challenge and personal growth then become an outcome of their achievement.

What role, then, does worker participation play in setting and achieving difficult work goals? The long history of interest in worker participation as motivator of high performance was carefully examined in numerous of these goal setting research efforts to observe its effect. They revealed no differences between performances on goals assigned top-down by the manager versus those developed with worker participation. Nor was there any evidence that differences in personality, education, age or gender had any significant influence on performance. Where such differences did influence performance output, they appeared to largely or wholly be overwhelmed by the effects of specific, difficult goals supported by performance feedback.

The role of the manager in the workplace was a critical exception. The quality of a supervisor/manager interest and involvement in the goals set was sometimes observed to be very important to the success of goal setting as a production motivator. Goal setting with logging crews, for instance, raised productivity only as long as the supervisor worked on the job along with employees. Having an interested boss working alongside probably produced a focusing effect. This quality of influence may go unnoticed in those settings where work is already supervised directly.

The lesson from goal setting with logging crews points up the importance of the relationship between crew and boss and the social context of work. The manager has a direct, personal role in efficacy of goal setting. Workers who respect their supervisor value their reputation with him/her. They do not want to appear lazy or uncommitted to the work that is their livelihood. They are being paid a wage to produce. Their choice is between putting a sharper focus on their work to gain efficiency or to relax and coast. That they are compensated for the work they can do and know how to do is sufficient incentive to do the minimum to justify employability. Goal setting provides the focus that concentrates attention, directs action, mobilizes effort, generates persistence in the work across time and opens the worker to discovery of better, more efficient ways to perform the task. As a form of competition with others working at similar tasks, it can add interest in work and invest it with purpose. Feedback about performance provides a game score that keeps it all going. The ability of the manager to arouse and maintain commitment among workers is central to the efficacy of goal setting. Goal setting can enlist the social process that generate mutual commitment and yields something close to the level of productivity inherent in workers' capabilities. The world rarely offers up simple, uncomplicated solutions to its problems. Goal setting seems to be one such discovery.

THE LARGER ROLE OF WAGES

Wages can be more important than just being basic incentive to show up to work and "do your best". They are significant in that they can both raise and depress output. When tied directly to output through piecework rates, or indirectly through group profit sharing schemes, money has been shown to be a powerful incentive to high productivity. Frederick Taylor demonstrated that piece work wages can motivate high productivity. In the studies carried out by Locke et al, piece work rates were found to be independent of goal setting as an incentive to perform at one's productive best. Next to goal setting, piece work pay is, indeed, the only significant alternative to goal setting as inducement of high performance. Of the two, significantly, only piecework pay has direct economic wage cost and added administrative requirements. Pay is institutional incentive with a price. Goal setting is a manager's direct, personal lever on productivity.

Piecework pay is further limited to tasks that can be analyzed with time study methods. It requires extensive administrative support to work at all. Piecework rates that are insufficient or are suddenly revised may cause reduced productivity. There must be reasonable degree of mutual trust and commitment between worker and employer for piecework to work as an incentive. A piece work wage system, where used, must be transparent and not subject to arbitrary revision that raises production standards or reduces incentive pay. Workers must believe that they will be fairly paid and treated. Workers who do not perceive their pay to be fair or adequate are not likely to want to perform better than the minimum under any circumstance.

The problem of productivity depressed or raised by wage rates has been empirically examined as one of perceived wage inequity. This is a condition where perceived unfair or low pay is shown to directly reduce productivity and where overpayment raises output. Insufficient pay in any form can defeat high productivity. Workers who believe they are underpaid are less likely to accept and work toward high performance goals. Workers who believe they are generously paid may perform to a higher standard. Wages must at least be adequate when the object is to encourage high productivity. Indeed, in the broader scheme of wage fairness, workers who do not believe that their pay is "right" may adjust their production to reflect their estimate of a fair day's output for the pay received. A corollary is that those who are adequately paid may need clear, difficult goals to bring them to their full productive potential.

In the early 1960s Social Psychologist J. Stacy Adams summarized a series of field observations and laboratory experiments that demonstrated the phenomenon of pay inequity. He formulated his observations into a theoretical framework that he termed equity exchange. Overpaid workers, he suggested, will work harder to restore a sense of transactional equity. Underpaid ones will balance the scale by producing less. Out of its relevance to a variety of social behaviors, equity theory became a standard element of study in the field of social psychology. Because perceived equity is a personal, subjective process, Adams' theory is of little or no practical utility in predicting the behavior of a specific individual. Nevertheless, those demonstrations that he offered leave no doubt as to the reality of this phenomenon. Clearly it is either a trap or an opportunity awaiting the unwary manager. Workers who think they are exceptionally well paid may or may not become stand out performers. Those who take their pay for granted as adequate may be inclined to coast and just need improved work focus to achieve high goals. People who think they are being underpaid may work less hard and appear to do so for no reason at all. Perceived inequity has interesting and curious results.[12]

Typical of several experiments carried out by Adams was a simulated, easily replicable task that required subjects hired as interviewers to obtain survey data from people on the street. This design focused on effects of under-qualification and overpayment. A group of college student males were "hired" for what they were told was an ongoing research project that could continue for several weeks. They would approach people on the street and attempt to interview them. All were paid the same hourly rate for their work which was set to represent a fair day's pay for the kind of work involved. By randomized assignment before work commenced, some interviewers were given to believe that, although they were not adequately trained and experienced for this work, they would be paid the advertised rate anyway. Others were assured that they were fully qualified for the task at the set rate of pay. The actual work was performed over a two and a half hour period. Performance results were scored in terms of the number of interviews obtained in that time period.

Within this 150 minute work cycle the average number of surveys completed by "under qualified" interviewers was 40.5.

By comparison, the "fully qualified" group's average performance was 28.5 interviews. Slightly more than 40% differential in work output was obtained from the "overcompensated" as compared to the fully qualified interviewers.

A study of supermarket cashier/packer pairing practices revealed the cost of perceived inequity when pairs were mismatched on experience, age and education. All were compensated on the same scale of pay. Packers openly complained about being paired with "lesser qualified" checkers and admitted to working more slowly when mismatched. Differences in equity of pairing were measured in eight stores. Labor costs for those stores with most frequent inequitable pairings were found to be 27% higher than in those with more equitable pairing practices. Perceived inequity directly resulted in working less hard by packers, producing higher labor cost and less profit. Adjustment of work output by a worker to reflect perceived inequity can and does occur. Perception of pay inequity in the work place is a wild card that can become an influence on productivity without apparent cause or warning.

Armed with knowledge of the inequity phenomenon, the experienced manager can take some steps to find the opportunities and avoid the traps it offers. Some possibilities to keep in mind are these.

- When hiring less than fully qualified candidates in a tight labor market, it may be shrewd to pay fully qualified rate and emphasize the disparity of pay and qualifications. This may be especially effective at motivating focus in a job where there is an initial learning curve.

- A strategy of "selecting for potential" rather than immediate full capability could possibly unloose a burst of productive output and learning.

- Striving for cost control with obvious low wages may be inherently self-defeating of productivity with those who know they are underpaid.

- Paying at or above market and measuring against difficult goals may in some circumstances produce exceptional output motivation where the worker is made aware of the prevailing pay rates.

- There may sometimes be purpose in commenting casually to the well paid worker that "I expect more from someone at your pay level."

Knowledge and experience have the potential to prepare a manager to create a system of performance controls that gets results. Pay and benefits may be no more than incentives to be present on the job, ready to work. Pay can, under certain conditions and with particular worker dispositions, directly increase productivity for the manager who knows how to use it. For other workers, pay may be irrelevant or negative as an influence. Better yet, setting difficult goals and providing knowledge of results may drive the best performance available. When the individual producer lacks clarity of goals and does not get performance feedback, nothing may work. Motivational control has little to do with motivational needs or satisfiers. It is very much about fair pay, the right mix of effective incentives and the provision of a clear job focus that emphasizes results. Those are fundamentals of work performance control that must not be overlooked or ignored.

3. THE EXERCISE OF POWER AND AUTHORITY

The exercise of power from a position of authority rarely gets much explicit treatment in management how-to books. It is a difficult and sensitive issue that usually is pushed to the background. The reality, though, is that formal appointment to a position of authority in a work setting is for the purpose of directing and controlling the actions of workers. Becoming vested with managerial authority creates opportunity for its application when the need arises. It also creates opportunity for mistakes. The mere potential for use of power changes everything. Crude or inappropriate use of authority can make it difficult for a manager to later rise above poor beginnings.

For those who are subject to the imposition of control through authority, the manager who wields it is always dangerous. Like the mice that sought to hang a bell on the cat's neck, they want forewarning of its coming. The manager's behavior is scrutinized for signs that will give warning of impending power exercise. His/her every action has potential to influence worker behavior, whether constructively or mistakenly. Possession of the authority presumes that power will be used and control taken. It makes every word and action of a manager an urgent message. The experienced manager will have learned that most of the control needed to get the job done can be effected with clear instructions, clear, difficult goals, and subtle words and actions. The simplest cues can affect the necessary basic control. That does not rule out complexity and variety in the way that a manager's role is enacted.

Some bosses get away with flamboyant, free-wheeling exercise of authority. George Steinbrenner, owner of the New York Yankees baseball franchise, was noted for his impulsive hiring's and firings of managers and players. He was quick to criticize and to enact his censure of those who earned his displeasure. Anna Wintour, the editor of Vogue Magazine, as she was depicted in the movie,

The Devil Wears Prada, was a cross between a bondage dominatrix and a Marine drill sergeant. The brutally competitive nature of the business probably justified her role choice. Ruthless power use draws attention and demonstrates the power of sharp authority to focus attention. Swashbuckling management is limited to those rare conditions where ownership of the situation is near complete and keeping workers sharply focused gets the desired results. The newly appointed line manager who adopted the Steinbrenner-Wintour style will soon find the weight of authority laid on him or her by someone higher up. Authority run amok is a loose cannon on deck. The deft touch is much more likely to be effective. Typically, the best approach in using authority is thoughtful, just restraint in its application.

Learning how to apply authority requires a special discipline of mind and action that defers judgment in favor of inquiry and suspends action while broader implications of action are examined. The recently appointed president of my university and I once attended a conference where we planned to make a case for special classification of our academic programs. This association was my turf and I had long been a working collaborator with many of its members. At registration I met a colleague who was a key commissioner on the board we were to meet with. Our conversation was wholly personal and innocent, an expected courtesy on both our parts, but at a distance observing, the president assumed I had started our campaign with the board. He took me aside and dressed me down verbally for beginning negotiations without him. Was he fearful that I would take leadership in this meeting away from him? If so, I dare not bail him out if he were to get in trouble. He would now have to make his own mistakes. I had expected to help him by guiding his approach to the board. Now I would let him go it alone. His readiness to misunderstand my actions and motives made it too dangerous for me to do anything else.

Those new to authority, as my president was, frequently jump to its application for fear they will appear weak or indecisive if they do not. Lack of experience generates lack of confidence that makes for error. When discovering the art of control through use of authority it is best to acknowledge insecurity and uncertainty. Patience and thoughtfulness are called for as the structure and fit of the new role are worked out and tentative steps are taken toward experience.

How the role of a manager is played has long been the focus of behavioral descriptions of a manager's work. Early research on managerial qualities focused heavily on personality traits because the personality of the manager seemed so very central to role effectiveness. Qualities like integrity, humility, fairness and assertiveness were focused on because they seemed central to being effective as a manager. These descriptors are less those used by managers to describe themselves than they are the qualities desired by those under their authority. They are less descriptions of action than proscriptions for it. They are the elements of the behavior sought from those in positions of power by those they work with.

The more popular proscriptions appear and reappear in the leadership and human relations literature. A typical list is one of "The Top Ten Leadership Qualities", published in the on-line newsletter, HR World.[1] According to this article, a leader (manager) is a visionary who is disciplined in single minded pursuit of his/her vision. He/she exhibits integrity characterized by honest dealings, predictable reactions and controlled emotions. The proper leader is also dedicated, magnanimous, humble, open, fair, assertive and creative.

This is not an empirically derived description of managers at work. It is a model image, a hoped for ideal of the power wielder's role. It is every worker-subordinate's entreaty for the boss' behavior. Those subject to authority only want their boss to exercise supreme self-control and consideration in the use of that authority. The good boss, effective manager, revered leader must, indeed, be the personification of self-control. Decisions and actions must be thought through in advance to the greatest extent possible. Crisis must be anticipated and met with realistic alignment of priorities for action. An effective manager remembers his/her past actions and words so that future actions and words need not be grossly inconsistent with those from the past. Workers will remember the past and react to any unpredictability they encounter. Inconsistency can on occasion still be used for effect. Some degree of whimsy is useful in holding attention. When there is gross inconsistency the manager must intend and recognize it. Unintentional capriciousness can only create confusion. Traditional personality traits are insufficiently well defined to get at issues like these. In a later chapter, the usefulness of newly empirically defined personality traits in selection decisions will be revisited. Management literature in general, though, has yet to catch up with what are now more standardized personality trait definitions. It continues to use the broad and poorly defined abstractions to proscribe the "good" manager's behavior.

The practice of managerial control is a craft that requires self-discipline. The fundamental rule for effectively controlling others in the work place is that self-control must be exercised in all matters that involve use of authority. Specifying the role of the manager begins with self-control, which becomes of utmost critical importance in the application of formal disciplinary measures. Disciplinary processes that spin out of control can undercut even the best effort to build commitment and maintain productivity. Fortunately, there are rules for assuring fair, effective discipline. For disciplinary action to support the missions of control, commitment and productivity, it must be applied as the practice of disciplinary due process. A grasp of this disciplinary due process is fundamental to the role of every manager.

THE PRACTICE OF DISCIPLINARY DUE PROCESS

Heavy-handed disciplinary action is a quick way to destroy worker morale and thereby invite a labor union campaign. A labor contract, if imposed through the NLRB election process, will almost always include the requirement that disciplinary action be subject to arbitration. When a disciplinary matter is entered into arbitration under a labor contract, justification of the action taken is put to the test of a professional arbitrator's judgment. Arbitrators are the equivalent of judges for hire. They are trained in the principles of disciplinary due process. Effective discipline under a labor contract must meet the test of established due process principles that can withstand scrutiny and be accepted as just. The manager and the organization that applies these principles before they have a labor union will likely build and maintain a reputation for scrupulous fairness with its workers that avoids labor unrest that might generate an organizing campaign.[2]

The first rule of disciplinary due process is that discipline may not be imposed on someone who has not been clearly informed of what is required and what is prohibited. Workers must have advance knowledge of those behaviors that can result in imposition of disciplinary action. Some actions may be assumed improper because they are wrongful in other social settings. Theft, intentional damage of equipment, falsification of work records, assault on another worker, do not necessarily require advance notice of their prohibition. As with any other form of banned activity, though, the facts and circumstances of even these wrongful actions may not be as clear as they initially seem. Serious as they might appear, immediate summary discipline is rarely demanded. Unambiguous establishment of the fact of the disciplinary infraction continues to be a requirement of disciplinary due process, however serious the offense.

Advance notice of those actions that can elicit disciplinary action must be supported with some form of explicit, formal communication. Many employers put work rules into print in the form of an employee handbook or notices on bulletin boards. That is not always the best approach, and labor lawyers may advise against formal written handbooks that could be interpreted by the courts as a binding contract of employment. Group meetings where production processes or market conditions are orally discussed can be a useful occasion to remind workers of prevailing work rules and offer some explicit do's and don'ts. A face-to-face meeting with each employee can be the clearest and surest way to communicate work standards and rules. In addition to regular on-going discussions, this kind of talk should always happen at the time when a worker is first added to the payroll. The inception of the employment relationship is the best time for such formal communication because attention is sharpest to the information offered.

When putting forward work rules and specifying those actions that are prohibited, it is critical that the business needs that are served by the rules be fully explained. If work flow requires regular, punctual attendance on the job for efficient, cost-effective production, that should be made explicit. If wage hour law and inspectors require wage payment for every one-sixth of an hour for a certain class of work, and work begins the moment the worker actually enters the premises, it is important to stress the accuracy of time records and point out that they are a required legal record. If particular kinds of clothing can get caught in machinery or could distract fellow workers, it should be made clear that accidental injury or damage is the basis of its prohibition. Blunt pronouncements without supporting rationale can fall short of inviting commitment to their acceptance. An explanation should always be offered that puts forward the basis for the rule.

These considerations set the foundation for the second rule of disciplinary due process that a professional arbitrator will apply. This principle says that the rule must be relevant to the successful conduct of the business. There must be a clear business need and justification for the rule that calls for disciplinary response. Rules for the sake of exercise of control stand out for their arbitrariness. Rules that support good social order in the workplace or that support cost control, work efficiency and safety are clearly justifiable and acceptable. In the unmediated relationship between manager and worker, discipline for breach of a rule that fails this test will, at least, generate resentment. It then can become a barrier to full commitment and willingness to sustain high productivity. No argument is needed to justify adherence to a rule that supports a legitimate business need whereas enforcement of a rule that has no basis in business need invites denial and rejection of the manager's authority.

The third rule of disciplinary due process demands that care be taken to establish the facts of the rule infraction. This rule specifies that the pertinent event(s) that constitute the rule breach must be thoroughly and impartially investigated. Disinterested bystanders must be sought out and interviewed one-on-one. The actions of those involved leading up to the event must be systematically probed. Likely biases of observers must be taken into account in evaluating witnesses' accounts of the event. Every reasonable effort must be made to gather all relevant facts and then evaluate them dispassionately.

The manager who evaluates the facts that may become foundation for a disciplinary decision must take control of the situation quickly to keep it from becoming confused by conflict and counter argument. The parties to and observers of the event should be quickly calmed and separated. If emotions are running high as a result of conflict or injury, those individuals who are directly involved can be suspended, sent to a convenient holding area or sent home. Key witnesses should be isolated for interview before there is opportunity to confer, coordinate and contaminate their stories. It is rarely necessary to immediately assess cause or render summary judgment of guilt or innocence. Certainly, it is never necessary to fire anyone on the spot. Suspension from work should be the worst case action. Suspension can be easily reversed without rancor or embarrassment, firing cannot. A dispassionate approach to the investigation, indeed, demands avoidance of excess drama. Actions must be undertaken calmly and deliberately.

The fourth precondition for fair discipline is consistent application of the rules. This does not mean that when the rule is broken, the penalty must always be the same. Rather, it points to the need for evenhandedness in enforcement. Rules are sometimes written or declared at a level of excess strictness to discourage their breach on a lesser level. This can be a foolish attempt to buttress the rules with blustery rhetoric. Where the rule is written, for instance, so that a single minute of lateness to work is subject to penalty of lost wage time and only rarely is enforced, unexpected enforcement will be seen as whimsical and arbitrary. If failure to wear a required item of safety gear calls for a half day suspension without pay, but the rule is enforced only when there has been an accident, the rule mocks the priority of safety. Discipline for violation of a dress code only when there is customer complaint renders the code symbolic. If the literal rule is not, or for practical reasons cannot be enforced consistently, the question becomes one of where the line is, in fact, drawn. Excess wiggle room in the rules themselves muddies the issue of whether or not there has been a punishable infraction. The line that must not be crossed has to be clear.

There is always room in the penalty decision to adjust to the circumstances of the rule infraction. The flexibility that is offered at that stage of the disciplinary process is covered by the fifth rule which says that the penalty imposed for breach of a rule must fit the situation and the circumstances that pertain to the worker involved. The manager's personal judgment is invited at the penalty phase. It is at this point that he/she becomes the personal source of all pain and embarrassment inflicted on the rule violator. It is appropriate now to think ahead to future disciplinary situations involving the same rule and ask if the penalty being considered would be appropriate to other persons and situations that might arrive at this same point in the disciplinary process. The temptation must be resisted to punish out of anger or come down hard to establish one's authority. Lesser penalty at a later time in what appear to be near identical circumstances will render the earlier decision unjust.

Differentiation in circumstances, though, is appropriate, necessary and important to maintaining the manager's control and authority. Care should be taken to evaluate small differences in the motivation for the infraction like the worker's attitude toward the work rules and his/her overall contribution to workplace efficiency and productivity. Disciplinary penalties can and should differentiate such circumstances in clear but subtle ways. Even a very small measure of inconsistency and whimsy can be permissible if discrepancies are carefully moderated. Indeed, the best strategy at the point where disciplinary penalties are to be set is to always apply the minimum penalty that is appropriate.

LEVELS OF DISCIPLINE

By order of severity, formal workplace disciplinary measures begin with a verbal, unrecorded notice or warning such as "you should not have done that." At the next level a written warning may go through successive stages that include a temporary record in file, expunged for good behavior. The next level is a permanently recorded written notice. Serious penalties start with suspension from work with loss of pay ranging in length from part of a day to several weeks, then move up to indefinite suspension, and ultimately arrive at full separation from employment.

The soundest policy for setting disciplinary punishments is to start minimally, then escalate, slowly and cautiously. Invoking a penalty that appears overly harsh will almost certainly reduce commitment and productivity from the disciplined person and possibly those around him/her as well. An overly harsh penalty can increase the likelihood of future violations and infractions by others who rebuff the action as arbitrary and deserving of challenge. The mere perception of excessive severity in a single instance can justify rejection of the rule itself. It has long been an established empirical fact that any criticism judged undeserved in a formal appraisal by a worker will result in a term of diminished productivity. The best criticism, the most effective disciplinary penalty, is laid on with a light, deft hand that persuades without serious injury to pride. Most importantly, these matters must always be approached without anger, impatience or fault finding. Good practice requires a degree of non-judgmental matter-of-factness that is contexted with assurances that it is the individual's actions, not his/her character that is unacceptable. Tempering discipline at a level of comfort for all involved will augment and preserve a manager's authority for the next occasion it is called for.

Where productivity is sustained and improved through control that develops commitment, disciplinary action is likely to be infrequent. When called for, however, it should not be avoided. The boundary of proper behavior must be respected and maintained, and its breach must be acknowledged. Allowing unacceptable actions to proliferate could create a break in the dam that cannot be repaired without a high cost. The best of all situations for a manager is a single, clear infraction that cannot be ignored. Quick, measured response to such a problem occurrence will gain respect and reestablish the limits of proper behavior.

When there is an outbreak of multiple infractions of the rules the worst possible response is to invoke mass disciplinary action. When this occurs, the issue of obedience to rules is already out of control. Bringing authority to bear on multiple offenders risks greater defiance. Where multiple rules breaches result from lack of regular enforcement, full and fair notice is necessary before their enforcement. A general announcement must be made that future offenders will consistently be subject to disciplinary action. Where there is concern that the issue is deeper than just sloppy maintenance of the rules boundaries, it is time to schedule meetings with all workers to assess attitudes and grievances that may be at the source of the problem. The only real solution may be to systematically set about to rebuild worker commitment to the organization and the work rules that are required for its effectiveness.

WORST CASE DISCIPLINE

Most experienced managers recall with regret at least one occasion when they applied more authority than was necessary or appropriate. This is one that occurred some years ago on the writer's watch. A newly appointed assistant foreman received a group of new employees for day long records processing and orientation on a Monday morning. These were workers in a heavy manufacturing operation located in an isolated rural area that for practical purposes was the only significant employer for many miles around. The work was quite dangerous and safety issues were heavily stressed. Impairment from alcohol or drug use was invariably enforced as ground for firing. With the aid of their labor union, first time offenders already on the payroll could sometimes claim that the presumed drunkenness was the result of a legitimate prescription drug that gave the appearance of drunkenness. Enforcement was thus seldom cut and dried. On this morning, a young local who had just come of age and been offered employment arrived for work reeking of alcohol. Asked if he had been drinking, he admitted that he and friends had been out late the previous night celebrating his new job.

In the strictest terms, this man had not been clearly informed of the company's rule against alcohol impairment. He was guilty of immature bad judgment in the timing and extent of his celebration, though by no means had he intentionally violated the rules. Someone more confident might have sent the young man home and told him to return for the next scheduled orientation session. Unsure of his authority, the assistant foreman conferred with the director of safety and plant foreman. Viewing the matter from a safe distance, they concurred that it was inappropriate to hire the boy and he should be sent away. The young man was crushed that he could not now go to work. Because he was not yet an employee and therefore not protected by the union contract he had no recourse. Rejecting him from employment before putting him on the payroll was the local equivalent of economic excommunication. It was a harsh penalty to impose.

Several weeks later, as the assistant foreman shopped groceries in the local supermarket, this same young man approached him. He pleaded for a second chance at employment. Imbued with authority yet uncertain of his standing in the organization, the assistant foreman firmly rejected the young man's plea. Labor was in short supply locally, this young man was clearly well motivated to be a good employee, and the request for a second chance was not unreasonable. This assistant foreman might have offered to look into chances for a new offer of employment and asked the young man to come see him next week. It was easier to say no.

What did happen the following week was appearance of a notice in the local weekly paper. The rejected young man had gone home that same evening loaded his shotgun and killed himself. The assistant foreman's rejection had, in fact, rendered a death penalty.

Giving authority to a working manager that can injure a worker's economic status has consequences, some grave. Every manager carries the weight of being a company marshal with the right to use economic penalty to stop or redirect improper worker behavior. Failure to use authority when it is needed amounts to dereliction at best, incompetence at worst. Presence of authority is fundamental to control in the work place. Every manager faces at various times the opportunity to use authority to either enhance or to undercut commitment and productivity. Skillful use of authority keeps everything in balance. Ineptly applied authority can wreck every other effort to maintain control, build commitment and raise productivity. It's a high wire act, the consequences of which can be daunting.

4. CONTRACTS AND GOVERNMENT REGULATION; UBER-CONTROL

Issues of authority and control in the work place go well beyond dealing with the immediate worker-manager relationship. Control is limited in part by the value of the worker's skill. The market value of that skill establishes the relative negotiating power of the parties to an employment contract. Workers who have rare or valuable skill can name their wage and working conditions -- up to a point, at least. Entertainment celebrities, sports idols, stand-out performers in most professions typically work under a negotiated contract that expressly establishes wages and working conditions. Social status and importance can also confer increased employment security. College and university professors as well as many public school teachers are protected from arbitrary dismissal under tenure, earned usually after a period of years of successful teaching or research performance. Those of lesser social status like factory laborers and service workers typically lack economic power relative to their employer. Workers can, however, organize under provisions of modern labor law and negotiate a contract with the employer that defines wage structure, working conditions and employment rights. The creation of a union with the potential to collectively withhold workers' labor can redress in part the relative imbalance of economic power between workers and their employers. Implied contracts in one form or another can also modify the extent of authority control exercised by the employer over the worker, especially as it pertains to employment security.

Most workers have little or no protection from arbitrary firing, members of management included. The typical solo laborer or worker looks mostly to government for regulation of the employment relationship. That creates whatever bargaining power he/she may possess. The foundation of all employment regulation is The Fair Labor Standards Act of 1938, since much modified, which sets the minimum wage for most kinds of wage work and established he requirement for overtime payment for work beyond the standard forty hour work week.

For well over one hundred years US workers have also been subject to the legal doctrine of employment "at the will" of their employers in matters of employment security. US case law as developed in nineteenth century courts established the presumption of Employment at Will as an employer's entitlement. Dating from an era of free-wheeling laissez faire capitalism, this doctrine holds that an employee not otherwise protected by actual or implied contract may be fired for any reason or no reason at all. Because of its long standing status as settled case law, it is the underlying foundation of every employee's non-contractual employment relationship, including the jobs of working professionals and managers. In most US States, if the employer explicitly announces a policy of employment at will as a condition of employment, workers have little or no recourse in the event of arbitrary dismissal from employment. Eleven states and a rare few employers including Federal and some State governments, operate within an established policy of separation from employment only for cause. Most private sector workers continue to be subject to at-will case law.[1]

The liberalizing force of twentieth century politics has imposed some modifications for some workers as an overlay on at-will employment in the wider economy. Since 1964, Federal laws have defined as wrongful those discharges from employment that can be shown to be based on race, religion, age, sex and national origin. In a variety of other ways the relative harshness of at-will employment has been muted. Decisions in the courts of forty three states have accepted the argument that adherence to public policy overrides the at-will rule. Under this rule employees may not be fired for performing their moral or legal duty. The typical application would be that case where an employer fires an individual for reporting their employer's illegal or fraudulent acts to the authorities. It would also prohibit separation for unwillingness to commit perjury on behalf of the employer. The burden of proof to show that the public policy exception applies will usually fall on the worker. At-will employment is modified, not eliminated.

The courts of thirty-eight states now recognize the argument that an implied contract exception to at-will employment may exist. At-will may be over-ridden by assurances offered in an employment advertisement or interview, spelled out in writing in notification letters, posted on bulletin board memos or published in an employee handbook of rules and regulations. Where they can be shown to have been offered, such promises and inducements to employment may be interpreted as an implied contract of employment that can only be terminated for cause. The matter remains subject to settlement by the courts, and, again, the worker takes on the burden of proof in those proceedings.

The courts of eleven states go still further to recognize presumption of a covenant of good faith in all employment relationships. For practical purposes at-will employment has been superseded in these jurisdictions and replaced by an expectation of good faith and fair dealing in every employment relationship. Arbitrary discharge that is not administered according to the principles of the disciplinary due process is subject to challenge in the courts in these states.[2]

Modifications of the at-will employment doctrine have been established entirely through litigation in the courts. They are thus subject to challenge as a form of judicial activism. The doctrine of at-will employment, however, was itself the product of judicial decisions rendered in the political climate of dominant laissez faire capitalism. At-will employment is not established or protected by legislation. It has simply grown out of the economics and politics of the times in which it was earlier litigated. In the late nineteenth century the industrial revolution held full sway, producing great wealth and lifting large elements of the population out of poverty. The net benefit of relatively unrestrained management control of labor was sufficient to overcome popular resistance to arbitrary discipline. Labor unions were as yet illegal and had no standing before the courts. At-will employment policy was established politically as legal doctrine in one era based on interpretations of common law, federal and state constitutions. It was subsequently modified in another era based on extended interpretations of those same instruments. That shift reflected both a political shift in public opinion and a shift in relative market power of labor versus ownership.

The legal framework within which at-will employment arguments pro and con for are fought in the courts is largely based on and balanced between long established common law. These are laws regulating undue restraint of trade, and the US Constitution's fourteenth amendment guarantee of an individual's right to due process and equal protection under the law. Argument in favor of an employer's right of employment at-will rests on the argument that inability to fire inefficient or unneeded employees will impede change and innovation that is economically beneficial. There is little doubt that removing limitations on an employer's right to expand and contract its labor force at-will can contribute to business effectiveness and profitability in a competitive marketplace. The counter argument is that employment instability produced by absence of due process and equal protection contributes to social and political instability. Social instability can be equally destabilizing of the economy, thereby stifling the desired innovation and competition. From the late 1800s up to New Deal legislation of the 1930s, that conflict frequently took the form of labor strikes that could turn into full scale industrial warfare where military and private security forces battled the strikers. Great economic loss was incurred by all parties to these conflicts.

In the climate of the Great Depression of the 1930s the quality and extent of government mediation increased radically. Labor unions, long a part of the industrial revolution's economic fabric, had been consistently branded by US courts as illegal. FDR's New Deal legislation made union organizing legal with passage of the National Labor Relations Act of 1935. Unions became legal.

With the passage of union enabling legislation in 1935, the battle for control of the working place was substantially equalized. It was recognized as an adversarial struggle that required government as arbitrator. Processes were put in place that allowed laborers to petition for union status through a secret ballot election supervised by a government agency. The rules of fair electioneering practices were established and enforced by the government. Once organized, unions could collect dues, become well financed institutions in their own right, and participate in the political process. They could influence politicians, courts and public opinion. In the following decades, significant modifications to at-will employment eroded the long standing right of employers to pay, hire, manage and fire at will. The mere existence of labor unions and the right to organize changed the workplace.

Some continue to argue that the ensuing loss of control by employers and managers is bad for business and the economy. That attitude overlooks the opportunity to enlist the worker as a partner in pursuit of efficiency and productivity. Heavy handed management control invites resistance and distrust under nearly all circumstances. Workers can bring more value to the bargain than just attendance on the job if they are allowed to retain their dignity as valuable partners. Absent virtual total control secured through imposed subsistence wages or forced labor, there are always worker expectations for some accommodation by employers and bosses. Dismissal of those expectations as presumption invites defensive opposition. The rise and demise of Soviet Communism offered a stunning test of the failure of forced labor to create a stable economic system. Under Stalin, forced labor was virtually total, thereafter, always partial. CIA observers on the Soviet ground heard and reported laborers to say that "They (the government) pretend to pay us and we pretend to work." The absence of opportunity for some measure of self-control is anathema to commitment and productivity. Excessive control of workers is self-defeating.

Employers and managers who want high productivity from their work force must respond to the expectations of workers for accommodation. Many professionals in the field of labor relations today operate on the assumption that disappointment of those expectations invites organization of a labor union, and once organized, that same disappointment invites work stoppage by a union. The issue comes down to the choice of meeting employees on the ground of their expectations, or paying the price of labor unrest. The National Labor Relations Act put that labor unrest into the category of legal and refereed.

PROVISIONS OF THE ACT

The National Labor Relations Act established a quasi "supreme court" for labor issues, the National Labor Relations Board. The NLRB possesses broad powers to intervene and mediate in labor conflicts. In one abrupt upheaval of liberal legislation, passage of the National Labor Relations Act put at-will employment on a very short leash held by government bureaucrats. Managers and company lawyers were faced with a new, major limitation on their exercise of control over workers. The law presents a formidable barrier to arbitrary management action in the face of union organizing efforts. Initially, it stripped away many assumed management rights under the at-will doctrine. It was a game changer of the first magnitude.

At the outset of the new law, time was required to establish settled legal precedent that would define the rights remaining to managers in dealing with union organizing and contract negotiation issues. New knowledge and skill were required for dealing with the adversarial issues that characterize these processes. Subsequently, the manager who was unprepared for a union organizing effort would be at high risk for stumbling onto one of the numerous land mines in this new field of contest. Extensive knowledge and training is, indeed, essential if critical mistakes are to be avoided in meeting a union organizing campaign. Every manager today must understand how labor organizing works and what restraints he/she must accept in dealing with it.[3] [4]

The National Labor Relations Act establishes that the intent and purpose of government as referee is to encourage the practice and procedure of collective bargaining by protecting workers' full freedom of association and self-organization. The Act further establishes legal safeguards for the workers' right to designate representatives of their own choosing who will negotiate the terms and conditions of their employment and mutual aid.

In meeting the requirements of the law, managers and employers must satisfy the following tests:

- They must scrupulously refrain from interfering with, restraining or coercing employees in their attempts to organize a union, bargain collectively, or engage in any NLRA protected activity.

- They must not attempt to dominate the organizing process by offering support or assistance to employees in their efforts nor may they subvert the process by organizing a company union.

- They may not discriminate in favor of those employees who oppose a union or against those who favor one.

- They may not retaliate against employees who file unfair labor charges or testify against the company at NLRB hearings.

- Once a union is certified by the NLRB, they may not refuse to bargain collectively or to deal with the employees' elected representatives acting on behalf of workers.

The iron rule of non-interference and non-coercion is the requirement that no promises or threats may be offered, either explicitly or implicitly, that are intended to create sentiment against a union. Promises and threats are serious matters. In the face of clear cut breach of this rule, the NLRB may schedule an election even though fewer than the required minimum of signed authorization cards have been signed, or, in extreme instances, it may overturn an election won by the employer and directly certify the union.

A manager who is faced with an organizing campaign, thus, must exercise the highest degree of self-discipline in dealing with its emergence. The first sign of an organizing effort is likely to be the appearance of a printed union authorization card in or around the workplace. The threshold for declaring a union election requires signed authorization cards from 30% of employees who constitute the bargaining unit. Cards are fundamental and must be taken seriously. Their appearance marks the moment when extraordinary care must start to be taken so that casual or unguarded comments about a union are not made. Once cards appear, a sample of the card itself should be sent up the chain of command for review at the top and by company labor counsel.

The appearance of union activity, no less than the presence of an elected, certified union, means that the working manager's life has been ratcheted up several notches of difficulty and stress. He/she has now entered the realm of uber-control where every word and action must be measured. The foundation of control as self-control becomes an imperative, not just a good managerial practice. Things that must now be avoided can include inadvertent bumbling into possible organization meetings, casual discussions with employees about organizing or impulsively speaking out against a union. There must be no suggestion of spying on organizers' activities. Those places where workers normally gather outside work must be avoided on assumption that organizing activity will certainly be in progress. Informal discussions with workers about the union can be dangerous, whether on or off the job. This does not necessarily mean that the manager's views about the desirability and usefulness of a labor union are not permitted. When offered, though, such communications must be fully scripted and documented. Management has the right to clearly inform its workers that it deems a labor union as undesirable and unnecessary. However, even arguing the lack of necessity could be interpreted as a promise or threat under some circumstances, or, if the union were not certified, could become the basis of an implied contract exception to employment-at-will at a later time. The words used to explain management's positions must be chosen with care.

In recent decades, reasonably settled rulings of the NLRB have established the ground rules for management's response to a union organizing campaign. At the first sign of activity experienced labor counsel and labor consultants are usually called in to set up the counter campaign. The conventional wisdom of experienced counter-campaigners is that the first organizing attempt will be lost only if mismanaged. A certified labor union means major changes in the work lives of everyone. Some of those changes may be as undesirable for workers as they are for bosses. Workers, for instance, may no longer go directly to their manager to settle workplace issues. Labor law requires that such matters be handled exclusively through workers' elected representatives. Other restraints and changes can discourage the pro-union vote. Unions are a business in their own right. They collect dues to pay officers and staff as well as to finance political campaigns and other union organizing efforts, in effect, collecting a fee for a service. Organizers are sales persons who themselves work for a wage. Organizing rhetoric comes as much out of self-interest as from concern for worker's rights. Making these points has potential to turn enough votes to defeat the first organizing campaign. Assuming successful defense, at conclusion of the campaign a thorough assessment of the issues that gave organizing its earlier traction must be accomplished. Visible, significant policy and practices changes can now be made that will inoculate the workforce against early resurgence of the union bug.

An ancillary element of conventional wisdom concerning union organizing is that a company that gets is certified with a labor union probably deserves it. Success of a labor organizing campaign reflects a lack of sensitivity to the prevailing labor market and to worker's expectations for treatment. Simple arrogance in handling grievances, too much readiness to invoke and apply employment-at-will as fundamental management doctrine, the appearance of favoritism and unfairness in worker treatment, all take their toll on employee commitment. Excessive reliance on arbitrary control of working conditions and employment as the lever on productivity reflects a lack of understanding and appreciation for how best to enlist commitment to productivity. Ultimately it can erode worker tolerance for all top-down, imposed control. Once tolerance is lost, the union's arguments are more likely to be accepted as the answer. If the requisite skill and knowledge required to deal with worker expectations has not been developed by managers before a union campaign, it will certainly be demanded and imposed on managers afterward.

Control carries a cost when it is either too little or too much. Every explicit act of control is a reminder that behind a manager's attempt to control behavior in the workplace there is the threat of forceful coercion and restraint. The greater the control applied the sooner that threat becomes a burden for workers. Once threat is explicitly invoked it instantly comes to the forefront of every power calculus. The manager who arrives at the point where coercion and restraint must be used has crossed the Rubicon of control. He/she is now demonstrably dangerous. If available measures and means of control available are used judiciously, that reputation may be beneficial. Acting clearly to maintain necessary boundaries of proper work behavior will increase credibility. Acting in ways that look arbitrary or unnecessary to maintenance of a productive workplace will diminish it. When credibility is lost, control is lost and a union election may be the next loss. Precision in control requires care and thought. Whether it is an automobile on a slippery road or a supervisor with a testy worker, too much or too little risks failure. Every manager must discover the proper balance.

PART II:

SECURING AND
HOLDING COMMITMENT

5. APPLIED SCIENCE AND THE WORKER

The seeming simplicity and directness of goal setting as the path to increased productivity begs an important question: Why does it work at all? Simply instructing (or is it asking, or could it be challenging?) a worker to strive toward difficult production goals requires, at a minimum, his/her willingness to accept the instruction/ challenge to pursue the goal. Goal setting works so consistently that it begs the corollary question; what are the conditions under which it does not work? The most likely, maybe obvious answer is that goal setting fails to elicit increased productivity when the worker has lost any sense of commitment to the job or manager. He/she is apathetically "doing their best". If commitment is to be created and maintained the manager must know how to recognize and avoid the emergence of apathy or antipathy.

For most of the past century of management history that issue has been approached as the problem of worker satisfaction. In its earliest form it was framed as the discovery that the productive worker is one whose manager demonstrates concern and caring for his people. This assertion quickly produced a flood of research that probed for the causes and sources of worker satisfaction. The foundational hypothesis of this research was most often and fervently stated as a satisfied worker is a productive worker. From its inception around mid-century through to the mid 1970s the yield of published scholarly research articles addressing this proposition was well into the thousands.[1] Yet this mass of research produced very weak positive correlations between measures of satisfaction and measures of productive output. The bottom line is that all this labor failed to demonstrate how increased worker satisfaction could raise productive output of workers. Those more skeptical among scholars sharply dismissed the utility of continued research as fruitless. Nonetheless, job satisfaction-productivity research in major social science journals continues undiminished in quantity up to the present time.[2]

The science that originated this tsunami of scholarly conjecture was, at best, well-meaning and primitive. It started in a Chicago factory that manufactured electrical equipment for the telephone industry, Western Electric's mammoth Hawthorn operation. These studies, begun in the 1920s, were a tangle of purposes and methods that largely failed as competent science while succeeding extraordinarily as popular ideology. They are credited by many as the foundation of a new social science discipline, that of industrial psychology. The Hawthorne studies blazed the way and fed the fervor of an emerging movement toward more humane working conditions in heavy industry that continues yet. As if by social mandate, some form of discussion of this Hawthorne experience continues to be included in every industrial psychology text.[3] At one time, a special division of the Academy of Management was focused fully on recovering as much original Hawthorne data as possible through videotaped interviews of original participants. Relay room workers were located and questioned for details of their original experience. One of the original Harvard research interns who observed on site was interviewed live in an Academy convention session. Few research undertakings in the social sciences have generated so much futile search for some kind of ultimate confirmation and yet exerted such extraordinary influence as did those at the Hawthorne works. An appreciation of how and why the satisfied worker is a productive worker hypothesis came to dominate management thinking begins with an examination of the multiple research campaigns carried out at Western Electric's Hawthorne manufacturing plant. Indeed, the history of the industrial democracy movement can be said to begin with the Hawthorne experience. An examination of these studies demonstrates how ideological commitment can distort and misdirect well intended action. A skeptical, open minded approach might have earlier grasped how they actually illustrated the effectiveness of moderate disciplinary action and commitment building with workers.

Research into the influence of workplace illumination on worker productivity began at the Hawthorne plant in 1924 and continued through 1927 under the auspices of the Illuminating Engineering Committee of the National Research Council. This experiment was intended and expected to demonstrate the beneficial influence of electrically powered artificial lighting on factory productivity. The first Hawthorne hypothesis, thus, was that the well-lighted factory is a more productive factory. The study was most likely funded by the one or more members of the Phoebus cartel that controlled the worldwide market for incandescent bulbs from 1924 through 1939. There can be little doubt that the results were expected to lay a foundation for expanded sales of factory lighting to companies like Western Electric.[4], [5]

The lighting experiment was undertaken with sufficient discipline to qualify as applied science. Up and down manipulation of lighting levels was limited to those seasons of the year when natural lighting was deemed insufficient to support the best productive efforts of workers. Lighting changes were installed on Sundays, the non-work day of the week, so that effects would be fully experienced by workers beginning with Monday's return to work. At one point windows were covered to shut out all natural light. No effort was made to hide changes in level of illumination that were made. Supervisors and workers were fully aware that the level of lighting was being varied and that a research study was in progress.

As lighting levels increased incrementally from the base level of 4 to the maximum 36 foot candles of artificial light, measured work output appeared to increase. Then, when lighting was returned to the base level as a check on the experimental manipulation, output continued to increase. Over a span of three years in three different parts of the plant, much the same result was observed. Productivity, graphically plotted week by week as lighting level was altered, edged upward regardless of whether illumination increased or decreased. Output declined only during those periods when the adequacy of natural lighting dictated the study's suspension. The planned demonstration of the artificial lighting's benefit was a bust. Not unexpectedly, there was no published final report. The lighting industry, disappointed by this result, abandoned interest and withdrew financing.

This was, nonetheless, a result that cried out for explanation. Word of it spread through the scientific community. Harvard professor of industrial research Elton Mayo thought he had the answer. Workers, he said, increased their output when interest was shown in the conditions under which they worked, then let it drop back when that interest was withdrawn. On approaching Western Electric with his analysis of the events, he negotiated a partnership for conduct of applied industrial research in the real world setting this company offered. Over a five year span from 1927 to 1932 Mayo and Hawthorne plant management collaborated in a demonstration of the benefits of humane management. Management concern for the worker was tested as the most likely source of high productivity motivation. Almost from the inception of research results seemed to be conclusive and were trumpeted as such. The phenomenon was subsequently designated as the Hawthorne effect, and summarized in the claim that the satisfied worker is a productive worker. This hypothesis was picked up and proclaimed in the popular press. Later, more rigorous theorists challenged this hypothesis arguing that the Hawthorne effect is, in reality, cooperative behavior that may be elicited by the presence of almost any obvious, explicit research intervention in almost any natural environment.[6]

If the confusion is to be rationally sorted out, the record of Elton Mayo's research and influence on modern human relations practices through the Hawthorne studies must be more closely examined. That begins with the detailed report of the Hawthorne research, authored by Harvard professor Fritz Roethlisberger and Western Electric employee William Dickson published in 1938.[6] The most thoroughly documented element of the Mayo/Western Electric research involved manipulation of working conditions related to manual assembly of small electrical telephone devices in the relay room. One hundred sixty seven pages of fine print are devoted to description of these experiments in the summary report.

The relay room experiment extended over the entire five year period of the study from 1928 to1932, spanning the crash of 1929 and the onset of the great depression. For purposes of research "control", a separate room was established in which the work of a small group of women assemblers could be closely observed while their output was precisely counted with mechanical apparatus. This assembly work was, in fact, a subset of work done by a larger group of about 100 young women. Their work required manual assembly of telephone relays at the rate of approximately one per minute through a standard nine hour work day punctuated only by a lunch break. The Hawthorne works of Western Electric on the western outskirts of Chicago, Illinois, employed some 30,000 men and women, most of them immigrants. It was a classic early twentieth century example of a labor intensive factory operation.

Two experienced operators were selected by the foreman and asked to choose four others to work with them. Six women, all described as thoroughly experienced, willing and cooperative, were chosen for isolation in the test room. The experienced relay assemblers chosen had most likely achieved a level of manual skill that rendered the routine of assembling these devices near to fully automatic. In their isolated work quarters five assemblers supported by their materials handler were under continuous observation by one or more persons. Though the roles and identities of the research observers were never fully clarified in research reporting, they did function as quasi-supervisors who were "always friendly and supportive toward the workers". There were numerous other observers as well. Company officials up to and including the Plant Superintendent dropped in occasionally to observe. Visits by various "industrialists, industrial relations experts, industrial psychologists and university professors" were commonplace. The relay room was a carnival in a fishbowl.

Although the atmosphere of the room was said to be permissive and congenial it was clear from the outset that work output was exactly measured. The pressure for increased productivity involved no redesign of relay components, no change in assembly sequence, no added training. It could be achieved only if the workers speeded up the manual assembly process itself out of appreciation for being chosen to work in the environment created for the study. In hopes that this atmosphere would be conducive to increased work output the ladies were advised that they should work the way they feel like working. Nonetheless, researchers recalled that "the girls (sic) came into the test with a somewhat suspicious and apprehensive attitude ... they were never sure that they were not going to be victimized in some fashion or other by the experimenters or by management." Indeed, there were early problems.

During the first three months of the experiment, concerns were expressed over "excessive freedom" in the test room. These were likely raised by managers who dropped by to observe or by the foreman of the larger group who continued to function as the direct supervisor for these six ladies. The problem was described as "a lack of attention to work and a preference for conversing for considerable periods of time". Operators were no doubt testing the limits of the atypical permissiveness offered in this situation by chatting with one another as they assembled relays. They were working the way they felt by taking pleasure in talking among themselves while they executed their mechanical routines. Two of the ladies were identified as the major offenders and brought before their foreman to be reprimanded for excessive talking. They replied "we thought you wanted us to work as we feel." When no change was observed in the frequency of their conversations they were removed from the experimental work group for gross insubordination and excessive talking and sent back to their regular work stations.

Throughout this early period of shake-down in the room, the work output of the five workers was either static or declining. Clearly, researchers and management expected humane treatment to quickly yield increased production output and were disappointed by the results. Excessive talking was thought to be a factor that could defeat expectations for increased output. The extraordinary departures in freedom from supervisory control the study allowed almost certainly clashed with a larger work environment where tight management control was exercised over all aspects of work. Too much freedom among these ladies might incite resistance to management control in the larger work group, perhaps elsewhere in the plant. Knowledge of the study was widely known. Too much, perhaps, was too much.

Upon removal of the two offending workers from the test protocol, replacements were chosen by the foreman. Both were experienced and said to be eager to participate in the study. One of the two had recently become the principal wage earner for her family. Her productivity and that of the other replacement assembler immediately exceeded that of any of the original five ladies and far surpassed either of the two dismissed workers. These two women set the standard for work attitude and output throughout the remainder of the relay room study.

Over the full five years of relay room observation, production was continuously measured while a variety of work incentives were introduced by management and the Harvard researchers. Changes were sometimes implemented after discussion with the workers, sometimes imposed. Morning and afternoon rest periods were introduced. Food and refreshment was provided during breaks and lunch. A piecework payment system was implemented for this group that was attractive enough to be later demanded by a larger cadre of relay assemblers. When the work day was shortened by 30 minutes operators increased their rate of output to maintain their total level of pay. Thus more relays were assembled in less time and piece work pay maintained the prior level of pay. As a rule, production increased or remained stable with any change that was made, even when it involved return to the prior base condition. Happy workers, enjoying management attention to their work and working conditions, were steadily increasing their production output. Their research hypotheses vindicated, researchers and management settled into the routine of this study and spun off additional research projects. We shall return shortly to one of those projects.

The relay assembly room was a closely controlled experiment mostly in the sense of supervisory oversight, measurement of output and documentation by the researchers. A sincere, honest attempt was made by researchers to understand what was happening. Modern social science was still in its infancy and an expanded body of empirical research on worker attitudes and performance was yet to come. Because researchers mistook behavioral control for experimental control the methodology of science applied was itself seriously flawed . Tampering with the population make-up to improve the end result of research was an egregious error of method. Interpretations offered to explain the events observed were driven more by belief in the correctness of hypotheses than by control of the multitude of variables that were in play. Other than in the conscientiousness of observation and documentation brought to the relay room study there was never anything close to qualifying as science.

Absence of a practical grasp of the statistics available at the time and a certain amount of overconfidence in the meaning of the raw numbers seriously limited statistical analysis of the original relay room data. Forty-five years later Industrial Sociologists Richard Franke and James Kaul, enabled with computing power, produced the "First Statistical Interpretation" of the original detailed data. Analyzing the data with newly standard multiple regression methodologies they identified three major factors as the cause of such increases in output as may have occurred. By far the most powerful influence was managerial discipline - control that was exercised over workers' performance. Managers and researchers had made it clear they wanted increased production. Second in weight was the effect of an expanding economic depression that dominated the second half of the study time period. Workers were fearful of losing their jobs and worked harder. The third factor was the insertion of rest periods in the long, tedious work day.[7]

These conclusions make perfect sense. They offer basis for an updated reading of the events in Chicago. The Hawthorne plant was no country club. Working conditions were severe and employees had little recourse when disciplined harshly or unfairly. Labor Unions were still illegal and the National Labor Relations Act eight years in the offing. The willingness of Western Electric's management to entertain academic researchers' intrusion into the real world of cost controlled production says that getting the desired output from upwards of 30,000 day laborers was no easy matter. Discipline was tight and workers were of no disposition to give more effort than the minimum. The ladies who were initially drafted into the study did not trust this situation and were as yet uncommitted to the object of achieving difficult work goals upon commencing their assignment.

When these workers showed no inclination to go beyond their usual routine level of output, management acted, undoubtedly with researchers' complicity. Mild coercion in the form of a verbal reprimand was applied. Supervision suggested, not so subtly, that lunches would be withdrawn if there was no improvement. Lacks of response to this prod meant that either the study must be stopped or some stronger measure taken. The choice was to invoke discipline. The ladies who were identified as leaders of this resistance were removed, not just for insubordination, but, implicitly, also for inadequate output. The message to everyone, the three remaining in the test room and all in the larger group, was clear: this is about higher output goals. Two replacement assemblers were chosen for their willingness and commitment to play the researchers' game. As researchers and management demonstrated sincerity of intent to improve working conditions, trust was reestablished and commitment rebuilt toward the object of continually increased work output. From reports of their response to these rewards, workers expressed satisfaction with their work and working conditions, evidenced behaviorally by a decline in frequencies of absence. In this climate of "good feelings" the rate of work output rose during the first two plus years until it exceeded thirty percent of the original base. Thereafter it stabilized and remained relatively steady. Overall this is a result that can largely be accounted for by a combination of a clearly communicated requirement for high work output and the development of worker commitment to its pursuit. Management and supervision were fully in charge, demanding commitment to goals, offering piecework pay, rest periods, lunches and shorter work days as incentive. High output was expected, control was tightened, committed workers were found to lead the way.

Hawthorne has since been harshly critiqued by skeptical social scientists. Australian psychologist Alex Carey caustically observed that "gross error and incompetence in the understanding and use of scientific method permeated the Hawthorne studies from beginning to end". He noted that evidence contradicting Elton Mayo's "happy worker is a productive worker" hypothesis was suppressed or dismissed while that which supported it was accentuated and highlighted throughout the book length published report. Belief that all was due to worker response to humane supervision overwhelmed everything.[8] Skepticism aside, the larger world of interest stood by enthralled. In a 1941 issue of the widely read Readers' Digest, noted American economist Stuart Chase detailed the Hawthorne "findings" under the title "What Makes the Worker Like to Work?" He proclaimed enthusiastically "there is an idea here so big that it leaves one gasping." Hawthorne burst on the industrial scene to become mainstream management and social doctrine. It permeates much popular management literature and management practice up to the present moment.

Curiously, the touchstone of much popular argument for the happy worker hypothesis was not the well documented assembly room studies but, rather, the earlier National Science Council's illumination research. The simple consistency with which changes in illumination as said to increase productivity could readily and confidently be linked to the introduction of caring, concerned management. It was a claim that has captivated succeeding generations of management consultants and lecturers. Summarized in about two of the six hundred printed pages contained in the Harvard group's book length report, the illumination studies recounted the continued increase in work output obtained regardless of changes up or down in level of illumination.

Serious reconsideration of how this data were interpreted came eighty years after. In 2008, original data from the illumination studies, never before statistically analyzed and thought to have been destroyed, were rediscovered by a team of economists from the University of Chicago. Statistical examination of that data yielded the conclusion that "existing descriptions of supposedly remarkable data patterns prove to be entirely fictional." Because the data was fragmented over three different spans of time subtle manifestations of increased productivity in the raw data appear to have been over-eagerly interpreted. The presumed "findings" of the illumination study may have been without sufficient justification. [9]

THE INTERVIEWING PROJECT

One research program at Hawthorne did produce significant innovation in research methodology and industrial relations practices. It is almost universally ignored by everyone who has ever promoted the Hawthorne effect hypothesis. This was the rather remarkable interviewing project implemented by Mayo's student protégé and, later, Harvard professor Fritz Roethlisberger. Over the three years from 1928 through 1930, more than 21,000 Hawthorne employees were intensively interviewed by a new class of personnel specialists coached and supervised by Roethlisberger. [10] This massive interviewing project fashioned the data collection interview as research method and laid the foundation for many of those human relations practices that characterize the modern personnel department.

Interviews were conducted by a small group of Western Electric employees chosen for their knowledge of the work as well as for their social skills. The earliest conducted interviews were somewhat crude, brief, over-structured and leading. At the outset, interviewers used direct questioning to solicit complaints and satisfactions that pertained to the three major issues of interest; supervision, working conditions and the work itself. Interviews typically lasted about thirty minutes. With this approach a list of the anticipated issues was presented by interviewers and the interview concluded. Interviewers thereby shaped the content of the conversation with leading questions as interviewed workers followed passively. Answers lacked depth and tended toward bland conventionality. The interviewee who tried to offer comments that strayed off the interviewer's program was pulled back onto the subject. Opportunities for real spontaneity were missed.

This was untried territory. Interviewers had naively wandered into a realm of interviewing as research method where they were lacking, but open to, experience. In one of their regular information sharing meetings notice was taken of those occasions when interview subjects had put forward their personal concerns. A difference was apparent. Whenever the interviewer led with specific, pointed questions, answers tended to be "yes" or "no" and extended responses were "stereotyped". Interviewees who were given free rein exhibited spontaneity in their responses that offered interviewers a sense that workers' real concerns being offered. Interviewers concluded that they were defeating their purpose by imposing structure and leading these conversations. Their approach would have to be changed.

In the second year of interviews, an indirect approach was adopted and applied. The interviewer would explain the program's purposes and describe ground rules that assured confidentiality. Then he would ask the interviewee to talk about whatever was on his/her mind. The interviewer closely followed the conversation, showing interest in what was said, recording it all as close as possible to verbatim. The interviewer scrupulously refrained from interrupting or changing the topic, entering the conversation only when necessary to keep the interviewee talking and clarifying. Interviews grew in length from 30 minutes to an hour and a half or more. The written interview record is expanded by a factor of at least four. Employees were talking volumes. The sheer quantity of data made it necessary that interview protocols be analyzed and summarized by a separate and independent analysis department.

For purposes of summary the information obtained was divided into two categories; supervision and issues of plant or workplace adequacy. Problems not related to supervision like work flow, health and safety were investigated by appropriate staff from maintenance or engineering departments. Issues pertaining to supervisory practices or behavior were summarized and presented in the aggregate as discussion material in regular supervisory conferences. The very large number of employees interviewed in each department meant that individual comments about supervision were easily buried in the greater mass of interview data. In supervisory conferences complaints were approached as matters of policy rather than personality and employed as discussion issues addressed in supervisor training meetings.

To support this massive, near universal employee interview program, an entire new layer of organization, committed to human relations problem identification and solution, was inserted into the already immense and complex Hawthorne organization. The object of this new personnel function was to find and resolve problems. Indeed, many problems were identified from interviews that, according to the research report, were realistically addressed in a variety of ways. Researchers also encountered at least three other major effects of the interview program that had not been anticipated.

As interviewers descended on departments to meet and talk with employees, supervisors could not help but be made aware that their supervisory methods and actions were under a microscope. Subordinates were being invited to express their likes and dislikes about the boss. For many of the bosses that created a heightened awareness of their own supervisory behaviors and methods. The almost universal coverage of departments by interviewers removed any sense of personal targeting. Nonetheless, that outsiders were interviewing their workers inevitably generated some degree of apprehension. Supervisors began to think about, critique and modify their methods -- a fact they often commented on in supervisory conferences.

Indirect interviews opened interviewers themselves to unexpected varieties of human behavior on and off the job. Interviewing was a practice whereby they became intimately aware of a wide range of human experiences and concerns. The depth of insight available from an open, unstructured interview opened new windows for them on the human condition. There was a sense of having acquired a new skill of immense power that could be applied to a variety of problem solving needs and circumstances.

Most unexpected of all, perhaps, was the enthusiasm and enjoyment with which many employees participated in these interviews. There was clear pleasure to being asked for their opinion on all aspects of the job and company and pleasure with the prospect of contributing to improvement of working conditions. A sense of emotional release pervaded the opportunity to talk freely and openly with representatives of management. Researchers concluded that many employees "when given an opportunity to express their thoughts and feelings to a careful listener discharged in the process emotional and irrational elements from their minds". The Hawthorne studies morphed into industrial therapy.

Hawthorne was a watershed moment in applied social sciences. Its consequences continue to reverberate in management literature. Sorting the useful out from the ideological has required most of the intervening years. The long ignored power of Professor Roethlisberger's monumental interviewing campaign stands as the most scientifically productive outcome of that era. The power of the open, minimally structured interview regularly continues to be demonstrated in social science research. Those who employ it in personnel or managerial problem solving continue to find it a highly satisfying effort and a hugely productive information gathering tool. It is, indeed, a tool that can raise the productivity of every manager. That issue will be reopened in a later chapter.

The crudeness of the relay room research and the misdirection of its findings produced innumerable academic and consulting careers that were mostly about the ideology of industrial democracy. That same ideology spawned an entire industry devoted to survey of employee satisfaction on the job and programs for enhancing that satisfaction. Concern for enhanced worker satisfaction continues to a be mainstream priority of many management teams. The usefulness of that priority has been regularly challenged and deserves fuller examination. We now turn to that discussion.

6. THE JOB SATISFACTION CONUNDRUM

The flood of published research unleashed by positive news out of the Hawthorne plant is testimony to the attraction of enhanced job satisfaction as general purpose answer to worker motivation. Research programs in abundance were initiated with the expectation they would demonstrate that proposition as truth. The vast parts of results were disappointingly inconclusive. Some findings were modestly confirmative, some disconfirming, most positive but weak. The easy tendency, amply demonstrated by Elton Mayo and company, was to focus on the confirming results. Still, the pervasiveness of unimpressively feeble findings could not be ignored. Disconfirmations appeared in print about as often as did affirmations. This conundrum stimulated secondary level of statistical analysis intended to uncover the broader implications of this growing fund of research. Aggregated statistical inquisitions called meta-analyses of job satisfaction research first appeared in 1955 and have continued on approximately a once-a-decade schedule up to the present time, all with near identical results.[1]

A meta-analysis aggregates the statistical products of a large number of research studies to establish the average result and describe the range of findings. It is a large and complex undertaking that can involve scores or hundreds of independent research studies. That job satisfaction research meta-analyses have been periodically repeated is testimony to the tenacity of the Hawthorne hypothesis and the volumes of research it spawned. With stubborn consistency, they have regularly announced that worker job satisfaction and productivity co-relate only to a weak, essentially insignificant, degree. The conclusion of the first 1955 meta-analysis proclaimed bluntly that "it is time to question the strategic and ethical merits of selling to industrial concerns an assumed relationship between employee attitudes and employee performance."[2] It was a pronouncement that went unheeded. The presumed link between job satisfaction and productivity was not just intuitively impelling, it had been solidly sold in by legions of professors and consultants armed with findings from the Hawthorne studies. It would not easily be dislodged.

An understanding of the complexities that can enhance or diminish the job satisfaction-productivity linkage requires some sense of how each is measured for research purposes. There is only limited uniformity in the kinds of measurements used across these studies. Job satisfaction is usually assessed through some form of self-report, either by questionnaire or interview. A great variety of formats and question lists are employed according to the preference of each researcher. Most ask an assessment of the worker's overall satisfaction with job or employer and then ask for self-ratings on a set of specific issues like supervision, pay, benefits, and working conditions. Responses are typically pre-structured onto a five or seven point numbered scale, attached to descriptors like "very satisfied", "somewhat satisfied" and so on down to "very dissatisfied".

Productivity is measured in multiple ways. Where job satisfaction is measured for each individual worker, the supervisor's rating of performance is most often used as a measure of productivity. Other performance criteria may include peer ratings, self-ratings, quality records, grievances, customer ratings, and output in units produced or dollars of sales where available. All are expressed numerically for statistical treatment.

Inevitably there is a degree of crudeness in most of these measures that challenges the reliability of the final result. Although confidence in reported research results derives in large part from the size of the underlying research populations it ultimately stands or falls on wide-spread replication in diverse circumstances. No single research study can ever represent finality in the search for understanding of the satisfaction-productivity linkage. Multiple repetitions subjected to meta-analysis establish or debunk the phenomenon.

Given the importance of meta-analysis to the science of measurement, what, then, does it mean that research results are said to be positive but weak? Are findings pertaining to job satisfaction and productivity relevant to the day to day practice of managing a work force or not? It is necessary to go behind the screen of statistical analysis to find answers to these questions.

In esoteric statistical terms, the average correlation coefficient obtained with meta-analyses done between 1955 through 2001 is on the order of .15. That is not a percentage; it is a singular statistical index. The proper interpretation of this index in percentage terms is that approximately 2% (two percent) of the variance between job satisfaction and productivity is accounted for in the research data. Ninety eight percent is beyond grasp. In practical terms this could mean that, in a work group of fifty people, one may be actively pushing the production envelope because of high job satisfaction, or that four or five may be working a little harder, applying more skill or experience in performing their work, because they are satisfied. The dominating proportion of workers are moderately satisfied, "doing their best" at their daily work routine.

Meta-analysis starts with published reports that claim a range of results from somewhat positive to somewhat negative and calculates the average. The outliers on both ends of the range also have relevance to interpretation of the overall body of research. Studies have sometimes produced significant negative and positive correlations that diverge sharply from the average. The largest negative correlations could account for about 5% of variance. This suggests that higher production is associated with greater dissatisfaction. At the other extreme of positive findings something like 20% of data variance is accounted for. At this level, worker satisfaction may actually be an important cause of higher production, at least to some limited extent.

Results at the extremes of range are not necessarily accidental or unreasonable. It can be expected that variations in workplace conditions can occur that produce real positive or negative correlations of these measures. That being so, does it mean that indeed, there might be a causal link between satisfaction and productivity? The answer is "yes" and "no". And even if answered "yes", the problem of reversed causality remains unaddressed. Co-relation may mean that high productivity is the source of an increased sense of satisfaction, not that satisfaction leads to higher productivity. Correlation is not causality. Causality can work either for a correlational finding. Given this opportunity for confusion, job satisfaction may just be too complex to be the all-purpose solution to increased productivity Elton Mayo proposed it to be. Managed astutely, productivity can be sometimes increased, though not necessarily, by "making workers happier". Much more than job satisfaction is involved.

That said, job satisfaction cannot be summarily dismissed as inconsequential.

Aside from the limited influence of job satisfaction on work output demonstrated by meta analytic research, there remain real problems caused by dissatisfaction that may directly or indirectly diminish productivity. Absenteeism and turnover rates do, in fact, correlate moderately well and consistently with expressed job (dis)satisfaction.[3] Dissatisfied workers are more likely to skip a day of work as temporary escape from the job. They more often look for alternative employment. At the extreme of expressed dissatisfaction, those who feel trapped and unable to either skip a day of work or change jobs, may find a solution in organizing a union. That can be costly and problematic for an employer. Absenteeism can disrupt productivity, turnover can destabilize production flow and a union organizing campaign will likely have high costs even if not successful. And there's more. Dissatisfied workers who have direct contact with customers can sabotage the sale with poor attitude. Dissatisfaction expressed to fellow workers can be disruptive because it serves to spread the dismal mood. Dissatisfaction can be harmful to personal well-being. Satisfaction is an emotional state that has been shown to influence health and longevity. Dissatisfied workers are harder to manage.

A happy worker is easier to work with than is an angry one. And on and on. These are impelling arguments for managing smart to avoid or minimize worker dissatisfaction. They are not necessarily arguments for broad programmatic pursuit of enhanced job satisfaction across a work force in anticipation that it will raise productivity. Some levels and kinds of dissatisfaction may even be productive.

Indeed, there are clearly many circumstances where dissatisfaction is supportive of high productivity. The object of addressing job satisfaction should never be to suppress all expression of dissatisfaction. A very high level of satisfaction can be achieved by providing genuinely extraordinary pay, benefits and working conditions. The organization that can afford to do that operates in a non-competitive environment where it sets prices with little or no constraint. The reality of losing in any form of competition is disappointment and dissatisfaction with poor results. That kind of reality is experienced by every team sport, from little league to the super bowl, where at game's conclusion, one team and its fans are exultant in satisfaction, the other depressed and disappointed. Acceptance of competitive loss without dissatisfaction means that there will be little attention to growth or improvement. Satisfaction is not a single, always positive quality of sentiment. It is a subjective mental state that may result from receiving praise for work well done, from complacency in too comfortable a routine, or from rising above crisis or defeat. Dissatisfaction expressed with the quality of organizational support for improved work performance is a desirable response. Too much satisfaction can easily become self-defeating, too little can be dispiriting.

Satisfaction and dissatisfaction are emotions that drive behavior and shape choices. They produce a form of stress that can damage or depress or, alternatively, enliven and strengthen. Job satisfaction must not be ignored. Neither must it be obsessed over. It should be recognized and managed with tools available. These include an awareness that satisfaction is shaped by worker expectations, that expectations often arise from and are modified by the manager's actions and words, and that dealing with expectations requires a manager to ask workers how satisfied they are. The astute manager embraces opportunities to deal with job satisfaction issues by managing expectations.

EXPECTATIONS SHAPE SATISFACTION

Satisfaction is an elastic measuring rod that can vary widely from person to person as a function of subjective expectations for the specific situation. What satisfies one person can dissatisfy another. The desired level of comfort at work for one may be agonizing inefficiency to another worker. Personal standards and expectations set the bar flexibly. Much that has to do with individual, personal satisfaction is a function of what is expected. Because they are wholly subjective, expectations will vary from person to person. Good working conditions for one may mean long work breaks taken at will, for another it can mean accommodation of personal issues that allow for tardy arrival at work, for still another opportunity to learn a skill. Dealing with job satisfaction thus requires that worker expectations be constructively managed and anticipated. The words and actions of the manager have considerable power to set and shape those expectations. Commitments implicitly or explicitly made by the employer can be of great or of limited importance in establishing expectations. Failure on the part of the boss to keep commitments can be either a serious or only an incidental disappointment for a worker. Only the worker can tell you which is the case.

Workers come to the job with some expectations built in and develop others through formation of both overt and implied employment contracts that develop in the ordinary course of events. Though disappointed expectations certainly do create job dissatisfaction and are often their source, the question of how they are formed, changed and manifest is rarely addressed as a concern of the working manager. Fortunately, for present purposes, a body of knowledge and research that examines the effects of expectations on behavior is a part of the management literature that pertains to marketing and consumer behavior. Advertisers create expectations for satisfaction with consumer products through claims and inducements. Understanding how expectations influence consumer choices is part of the marketing realm of management education. A body of useful findings and principles exists there.[4]

The major difference between consumer satisfaction and job satisfaction is in the much larger number and frequency of opportunities available to the consumer to test his/her expectation for product or service satisfaction. Worker satisfaction is formed on the job over a longer time line with fewer, more significant tests. Consumer satisfaction usually, though not always, is superficial and fleeting. Job satisfaction can be fundamental to personal well-being.

Every normal, literate job seeker comes outfitted with a set of expectations for how he/she should be paid, how bosses should behave, how personal needs should be accommodated, or how secure their job should be. These can be intensely personal, private concerns. If not made explicit in pre-employment or problem solving discussions, they may become desperate, hidden hopes. Level of intensity will vary. Expectations can exist at different levels of personal urgency. Some expectations can be or should be, while others will be or must be. Many expectations will be implicit. The worker who expects an early pay adjustment or training opportunity may be mildly or deeply disappointed when it is missed depending on explicitness or implicitness of promises made or presumed to have been made.

The private nature of expectations offers opportunity for the level and intensity of expectation to vary significantly. Work expectations are continually being created by the political, economic and social environment that surrounds each individual. Friends exchange information on pay, benefits and working conditions in their various employment settings. News articles suggest standards that employers are expected to meet. Past experience establishes a personal base of expectation that can be especially resistant to change. Where the offered pay is significantly less than prior income, or where working conditions are less than desirable, dissatisfaction can be inevitable. A significantly higher pay adjustment for a co-worker compared to one's own pay level will create a negative comparison that shifts expectations. Comparisons with immediate fellow employees are most influential in setting expectations, comparisons with workers at a distance are less so. Each individual assesses the rewards and benefits of employment from all available sources and finds his/her own ground of anticipated reward. Some part of variability in expectations formed will be shaped by personal factors like self-confidence and ambition.

Expectations are created beginning in the first moments of an employment relationship. The earliest are likely to be assumptions about advancement beyond beginning pay and about the availability of long term work. Recruitment through temporary agencies is commonly used to preclude any expectation of a long term work association. Being put on the payroll implies joining the production team, being a "temp" does not. Being "hired" produces an immediate presumption of a stable, enduring work routine. At the outset most full time jobs with standard benefits are taken to be of indeterminate length. There is no specified contract end date. Because the point of termination is unknown, it will always disappoint individual expectations when it ultimately arrives without notice.

Employers are often complicit in building expectations for stable, long term employment. This can occur despite clear statement of at-will employment policy upon hire. Employers want new workers to come on board energized, excited, motivated to produce. It is implicitly assumed that suggesting any kind of time limitation on a career could depress motivation and distract from the work to be done. Enthusiastically welcoming the new worker on the job suggests the inception of long term work. Trial periods like job probation suggest that employment should last indefinitely once past the trial period. Pointing to the business' growing market for product or service suggests good job security and work without end. Emphasis on promotional potential raises long term career hopes. An extensive administrative hiring-on process and orientation suggests long term stability. Without any consciously formulated awareness of doing it, these measures can generate an implicit expectation of a job, without any termination point. Any later suggestion of instability in the work relationship will be unwelcome news.

Employers typically avoid emphasis on, sometimes even avoid mentioning, work rules, output expectations, disciplinary processes or competitive threats because of a misconceived presumption that nothing must detract from maximally motivating an employee's work effort out of the starting gate. The harsher underside of the manager-employee relationship is politely shielded from view. The more successful this charade is, the more disappointing ultimate revelation will be.

None of this need be. At the very outset, it is important for the working manager to establish realistic expectations about work. There can and should be a matter-of-fact discussion of workplace expectations for the new employee. Normal length of time learning the job, as well as its relationship to other work in the company, can be described. The likely challenges to be met in mastering work performance can be laid out. Common missteps and mistakes that could be serious or embarrassing should be detailed. The level of production efficiency typical of new employees can be made specific to establish the manager's expectations. The climate of competition in the industry and resulting pressure for cost control and high productivity can be clearly put on the table. Work record rules, confidentiality requirements regarding company information, prohibitions of relationships among employees, proper procedure for taking paid sick days, anything that could be a surprise when it later comes up can be made explicit.

A reality check discussion of this sort need not nor should be made heavy with suggestions of authoritarian control. It can be approached pleasantly and matter-of-factly. Drawing the boundaries that define the realm of expected and accepted job behavior doesn't have to be an embarrassed or solemn matter. The manager who orients workers to the work setting need not apologize for laying out real job requirements and stresses. A straightforward manner and a mentoring tone can be employed. When communicating rules, procedures and work realities, the manager must never frown, scowl or avoid eye contact. This is a discussion that should be rehearsed in advance with a good coach. The cost of messing it up with unintended negative cues could be high. Disappointed expectations are the primary source of most if not all job dissatisfaction. Overly negative expectations can generate dissatisfactions too. The manager must be aware of how his/her actions that can shape worker expectations in every communication offered.

Shaping expectations does not stop at the job entry point. In communicating with workers a competent manager will always work to master the essential skills of putting an expectation-constructive message across. Ineptly impulsive communication, off the cuff comments, not-thought-through promises, subtle suggestions intended as motivators all have potential to generate troublesome expectations. Spontaneous pronouncements on important issues should be suppressed or avoided to avoid expectation setting blunders. The potential for expectations that any communication might set must be anticipated and managed if the unwanted outcomes of job dissatisfaction are to be avoided.

Many issues of discussion can be opportunities to succeed or fail in managing worker expectations. Pay is one of the most important. If employees are told that pay adjustments are made annually and average around 3%, any delay beyond the exact anniversary date will certainly create anxiety and dissatisfaction A mere 2% increase will be a big disappointment as well. The better policy may be to announce that pay adjustments can occur periodically on no certain schedule and that they are a function of business results and worker performance. The annual basis will be assumed by most employees and anything in reasonable range will usually be accepted. Distinctly earlier action will likely exceed expectations, significant delay will disappoint them. In the context of no certain schedule, opportunity will exist for the manager to anticipate these responses and shape alternative expectations in advance. The manager will usually be a prime source of expectation generation for his/her workers. That is a reality that must not be ignored. Every announcement that pertains to pay, benefits, added work, competitive forces, future market growth, work rules, or anything else that represents possible reward or penalty must be considered for its influence on worker expectations.

Once aware of how expectations are generated and shaped, it should not be concluded that the safest strategy is to set modest expectations that can easily be met. Low expectations do not necessarily support high performance goals. Expectations that are easily met seldom improve job satisfaction and could suggest tolerance for low standards of work. Low expectations do not support managerial leadership in service of increased quantity and quality of productivity. Meeting modest expectations rarely offers any improvement in satisfaction. Exceeding low expectations may merely escalate expectations to a higher level without any gain in satisfaction. On the down side, setting low expectations runs the danger of generating serious job dissatisfaction when disappointment comes. Setting strategically low or modest expectations is "sub-optimal" expectation management strategy that offers little or no payoff.

The greatest risk and highest reward is in setting high expectations. High expectations disappointed are an emotional jolt. Major dissatisfaction will be the result. But when high expectations are met or exceeded a major boost in satisfaction can be the reward. An economically trivial but emotionally real illustration is found in the response of fans to the performance of their favored sports team. Energized and expecting their players to triumph in dominance, a major, if transient, bout of heated rhetoric and depression can follow loss of the game. A hard fought win will generate exultation. The worker who expects a large increase or major promotion can fall into serious despair when it is not forthcoming. A rise in expressed dissatisfaction will certainly be the enduring result. The worker who gets the largest possible expected raise will be happy. The one whose high expectations are exceeded will be ecstatic.

Some personalities absorb disappointment easily, others dwell on it. The manager who makes fair decisions will generate some disappointment. The calculus of what is trivial and what is major will depend very much on how well he/she knows workers as individuals. An ongoing assessment of internal dissatisfaction is always available to the manager who has the skills needed to relate positively and in depth with his/her people on a personal level. There will be few surprises. To avoid even those surprises, lingering and undisclosed complaints can be simply and routinely assessed through periodic attitude surveys. A periodic anonymous attitude survey is the simplest, least disruptive, most cost effective way to let workers tell their bosses how satisfied or dissatisfied they are.

JOB SATISFACTION SURVEYS

A periodic employee attitude survey can be a useful gauge on the manager's instrument panel despite the qualms he/she may have about exposure to criticism. Discovery of dissatisfaction need not be feared. Expression of a realistic level of dissatisfaction within any work group can be an indicator of communications honesty within the group. Expression of moderate dissatisfaction is a demonstration that the manager is facing the tough decisions required of the job. Questionnaire items that specifically tap issues known to be of concern will measure the extent of that dissatisfaction. Surveys, like the open interviews in the Hawthorne plant, can bleed off some simmering negative sentiment just because they are done. Full, candid feedback of survey findings can often then generate increased satisfaction. When survey results are honestly and openly addressed, a variety of benefits can flow from this simple, low cost data gathering methodology.

To maintain fullest credibility as to the trustworthiness of data analysis, it is often best to use an independent party to administer, handle and summarize the survey results. The plethora of research on job satisfaction issues over the past half century has produced spin-off in the form of a very large job satisfaction survey industry. Any internet search of job satisfaction surveys immediately turns up scores of offerings, many with tested questionnaires and a large bank of comparative data generated across diverse companies and industries. An independent outside organization can bring credibility to the confidentiality of survey answers and experience to its administration and interpretation.

Useful survey results do not require lengthy, elaborate questionnaires. They are obtainable from very brief, simple instruments. Overall satisfaction is calibrated with a "how satisfied are you with your employer as a place to work", or "how satisfied are you with your job". A simple five point scale that ranges from highly satisfied to greatly dissatisfied will serve adequately as the quantitative answer. Specific questions can address matters like accessibility of necessary supplies and equipment, availability of mentoring or training, solicitation and acceptance of workers' ideas, supportiveness of supervisor, fairness of criticism and discipline, significance of individual work effort, quality of relations with co-workers, etc., etc. Most of the time, the same five point answer scale can be made to work with all questions. Clearly framed as declarative statements and simply measured on a numeric scale, the results will be easy for everyone to understand. Any questionnaire instrument used must avoid leading questions or unwise suggestions of impending policy revision. A question like "are raises adequate" or "should company rules be changed" could raise expectations for policy revision. To be safe, the questionnaire can be reviewed by managers experienced with surveys and by company legal counsel to assure that nothing is asked that would be improper or likely to create disappointment.

Interpreting the data need not be complicated. Some dissatisfaction is normal and expected. The absence of any expressed dissatisfaction should be suspect. The most positive attitudes I have ever seen were from a group whose hyper-defensive manager was unwilling to accept any criticism. On being interviewed his crew unanimously confessed that he would be impossible to work with if criticized. They knew better than to be candid. One of the harshest expressions of job dissatisfaction ever was obtained from a work group whose work habits and productivity had become unacceptable as a result of former lax supervision and standards. A personable young management trainee on temporary assignment had effectively corrected the problem with tough oversight. Workers knew they had to accept higher standards, but hated it anyway. Expression of dissatisfaction on the survey was useful bleed-off of strong sentiment.

Satisfaction data can provide internal comparisons with other worker groups that give meaning to the overall pattern. Routine correlations of specific items to a statement of overall satisfaction suggest where the hot spots may be. Some survey firms provide comparative data for similar businesses or industries. The Pew Research Center for Social Trends publishes new and historical job satisfaction data on its web site. Over the span of a two decade corporate career in General Electric I designed or was closely associated with more than three hundred job satisfaction surveys, some with unionized workers and several covering tens of thousands of employees. The rule of thumb I used for interpretation of overall dissatisfaction percentages was that hourly workers typically express some or much dissatisfaction in the range of 15% to 25%. For salaried staff that range is 5% to 15%. At and beyond the upper limit of these ranges there may be cause for concern. In most surveys there are likely to be one or two specific problem issues. After every job satisfaction survey, those can be identified and addressed. By providing visible, well publicized fixes to the most pressing specifics uncovered by a survey, dissatisfaction can often be tamped down.[5]

Much like at the Hawthorne plant, working managers whose peoples' sentiments are being solicited in through interview or survey can feel uneasy, even threatened. Some may object strongly to this as an unnecessary power reversal device. Personal sensitivities aside, regularly conducted job satisfaction surveys can provide managers with incentive to develop the sensitivities and skills that permit them to become more fully informed about workers' interests and expectations. Argument can be made that those sensitivities and skills are central to effectiveness as a manager and that their lack is a grave weakness. The manager, who masters them, can quickly and effectively solve the problems of job dissatisfaction and problematic expectations that exist in the workplace. Proficiency with open interviewing techniques will also serve this purpose by providing a foundation for adjustment of work and organization practices to meet worker needs and preferences. The skills and processes involved in such interviewing will be addressed subsequently.

Although worker job satisfaction is unmistakably relevant to productivity, the happy worker is not necessarily a committed worker who can be focused on productivity goals. But without some minimal measure of overall satisfaction, commitment to any goal beyond a regular paycheck can be illusive. Dissatisfaction that is at the edge of being serious or epidemic portends major problems. Keeping dissatisfaction within an acceptable range is a part of every manager's job. Satisfaction alone is not enough. Once achieved, it can be the foundation on which commitment is built and maintained.

7. PARTICIPATION, SATISFACTION & COMMITMENT - IT'S COMPLICATED

The effective manager knows how to use the levers (variables - in research terms) that are critical to productivity and ignore those that are not. Frederick Taylor identified two of them, standards for work and clearly set goals. Taylor designed the most efficient sequence of work and timed the task to calculate an output standard. Workers were then trained in performing the task and expected to meet the standard. Pay was strict piecework and determined by quantity of output. It is an approach to motivating productivity that, while it seems fair enough, can generate strong resistance among workers, especially those represented by a union. When implemented at the government's Watertown Munitions Arsenal, Taylor's approach generated a political storm at the highest level of government. In 1912 he was forthwith summoned before members of the Congressional Commission on Industrial Relations to defend his system and methods.[1]

Taylor's methods increased productive output and often also produced vocal job dissatisfaction. This served to demonstrate the obvious, that productivity can be increased without job satisfaction. Nevertheless there can be little doubt that sufficient job dissatisfaction will increase levels of worker absenteeism, turnover and union sentiment. Taylor's approach achieved management's production goals without generating worker commitment to its goals. He put workers in a vice and dared them not to be productive. Like an engine operated without lubricant, this approach can be a noisy, friction plagued process.[2]

By contrast, goal setting, a close parallel to Taylorism, has potential to achieve essentially the same objectives as Taylor's with little or no complaint or resistance. The distance from Taylor's scientific management to Locke's goal setting seems at once trivial and huge. Finding the path from one to the other would appear to be the trick. Rebuff vs. acceptance of standards is the most likely difference. Committed workers embrace standards set by their manager, uncommitted ones do not. Lack of worker commitment can explain rebuff or acceptance. Commitment accepted is the foundation of high productivity. Commitment rebuff yields mediocrity.

Management research literature in recent decades has begun to move toward more emphasis on building commitment in the work force to explain productive behavior. Sometimes the preferred expression is engagement. Both commitment and engagement make reference to some form of emotional connection with the job and work goals. Emotional disconnect is rebuff, emotional connection is commitment/engagement. Workers who are willing to voluntarily pursue difficult goals set by their manager are those who have not yet abandoned their commitment to or engagement in the job.[3]

Commitment is a complex emotional thing. It is, at minimum, attachment, adhering, faithfulness, dedication. In an organizational setting such attachment can occur at multiple levels. One can be committed to the organization as an instrument of one's personal objectives. Commitment can be to ideals, beliefs, friends or family. Commitment to one's manager and fellows can emerge in the face of threat, mutual need or pursuit of high ideals. Commitment comes in various sizes and shapes.

Most commitment to work goals arises out of shared purposes in achieving economic security. Most workers arrive at the workplace ready to do what they were hired to do, pre-committed to boss, job and company. Commitment is offered in good faith with the expectation that it will be honored and rewarded. At its inception a worker's commitment are the manager's and the organization's to be maintained or lost. It will be lost when expectations for respect, honesty or fairness are disappointed.[4]

The always subjective, unpredictable quality of personal experience means that commitment can easily be dashed for some workers even as it endures stubbornly for others. Either way, there comes a point at which the good will underlying commitment begins to dissipate. Once commitment is lost, the choice of manager (and management) is to tighten control to compel goal achievement, or reenlist whatever engagement remains to rebuild commitment. Rebuilding, clearly the superior choice, takes skill in application of the manager's craft.

One very popular recommendation for rebuilding lagging or lost commitment has been to enlist employee participation in making those decisions that shape their jobs and working conditions. Empirical research has offered some mixed encouragement to those who embrace participation as the solution. There is at the outset a problem of definition. Like job satisfaction, participation is a loosely defined construct that encompasses a variety of independent variables. Understanding what is going on requires that we go deeper into the processes that are termed participative.

At the most superficial level participation may involve only passive acceptance of management decisions made while "participants" merely stand by watching. At the most dynamic it can become provision of opportunity for workers to make important business decisions and direct their implementation. Neither of these descriptions makes reference to any kind of emotional involvement in the process. Attachment and rebuff have been ignored. If the difference between Taylor's scientific management and Locke's goal setting method is to be bridged, the emotional responses that emerge through participation must be referenced. The multiplicity of elements that define participative behavior must be analyzed for the passion evoked in the response of participants. Revisit of a well documented, widely referenced mid-century research study of worker participation can illuminate how those passions emerge.[5]

In 1947, two years into the post World War II economic boom and a decade beyond the book length publication of the Hawthorne chronicles, another landmark research study appeared. Focused on worker participation it was titled "Overcoming Resistance to Change." Without apparent intention on the part of researchers Lester Coch & John French, the conditions that characterized Frederick Taylor's theory of productivity were closely paralleled in the Coch and French research design. Both used real work in real companies with real employees, Taylor at Midvale Steel near Philadelphia, Coch & French at Harwood Manufacturing in the mountains of Virginia. Both established task structure and trained workers in task performance, both set clear output standards, both paid output on a piecework basis.

The half century between demonstrations of these highly similar productivity enhancement methods was bridged at Harwood by inclusion of a control group that closely imitated actions taken at Midvale. Observation of research interventions with control and experimental groups at the Harwood site were documented and reported in considerable detail. Methods and results of both have subsequently been critiqued numerous times. Harwood method and results can be examined and reinterpreted from the available documentation, even at a distance in time.

The Harwood company manufactured pajamas for the commercially competitive dry goods markets. The plant was located in the small town of Marion, Virginia in the state's rural southwest highlands more than a hundred miles from any major city. Most employees were young women with grade school or less education and no prior industrial experience. Production jobs were designed by industrial engineers who set the standards for expected hourly production in every job. Piece work pay based on these standards was in effect throughout the plant. Efficiency standards developed for defense production in World War II were the norm as well. Work tasks were highly repetitive manual routines.

A commodity item like pajamas is continually under price pressure for cost reduction. As post-war demand for goods accelerated, the intensity of cost pressure on Harwood was unremitting. Industrial engineers, practicing a discipline less a science than a high art, were under constant pressure to come up with ever more efficient production processes that eliminated labor time and cost. Task elements of a job would be combined, cut or rearranged, a new time standard set and workers retrained. Before long the process would begin over. Workers would establish one routine that permitted standard piecework rate to be achieved, and then be subjected to a change of routine that required them to learn a new routine and achieve a new production standard. Most such changes eliminated no more than 10% of the original job routine. Though changes were minor and the end purpose of the task largely unchanged, the average "relearning curve" was eight weeks. To offset lost piecework wages during relearning and recovery of earnings, workers were paid a "change bonus". The usual reaction to changed piecework rates was vocally expressed dissatisfaction by operators about having to perform to the new rate. Weeks of struggle were required to raise production to the new standard. The stress of change was sufficiently severe for operators to frequently express their rebuff by refusing to meet it. The whole exasperating episode was all too frequently cut short when the worker quit her job.

Harwood was unusually supportive of its work force. It provided a minimum wage floor to employees who fell short on piecework for any reason. Health services and recreation programs were offered all employees. In a limited local labor market where a reputation for poor working conditions would spread quickly, dissatisfaction and high turnover were direct threats to productivity. Replacement workers could be hard to find, and grievances filed through the labor union could be time consuming and costly to handle. Harwood applied a variety of progressive employee practices to overcome these challenges. Social science research was one of those practices.

Management at Harwood was nonetheless unrelenting in its insistence that workers meet performance standards. Work output was calculated every day and published the next morning in rank order from highest to lowest producer. The output report listed by name was shown to every operator. Work was tedious and subject to the rigorous quality checks required of a consumer product. On some tasks, the average new employee might take up to 34 weeks to acquire the skill necessary to perform at the engineered standard. These young ladies, average age about 24, were subjected to a production pressure-cooker. For their age and education, though, they enjoyed good, high paid jobs.

To find answers to the stresses and resentment change generated, Harwood management asked University of Michigan psychology professor John R.P. French and his colleague Lester Coch to examine the change process. The researchers began with the presumption that worker participation in the design and implementation of a redesigned task and piece rate would raise "morale" enough to carry operators through the difficult process. They set forth to demonstrate the power of participation by changing the way tasks were reengineered and piecework rates were introduced.

Four intact work groups were chosen for experimental treatment. All workers in each group were performing the same routine, standardized, time engineered task. Any change in task design or standard rates would affect everyone in the group. One group was chosen to represent the control condition of the experiment. The other three groups consisting of thirteen, seven and two people respectively, were to get the experimental treatment. The four groups were said to be roughly matched on pre-existing efficiency ratings and the extent of task change to be introduced. The observed closeness of informal personal relationships within groups was also matched since intact work groups were known to develop relationships that could amplify either resistance to or acceptance of task and standard changes. As another point of match, the control and the larger experimental group shared the same supervisor. For an experiment in a field setting where randomization was impractical, matching of group composition was at least adequate.

The control group got the prevailing treatment. Using observed standard task times, industrial engineers eliminated or modified task elements deemed "frills" and set a new, tighter time and piece work rate. Against this rate, workers would have a little less work to do, usually about 10% less, that could be performed in less time, thereby cutting labor time and cost. Once the revised task and rate were approved by production management the work group was convened and informed of the change. The existence of competitive forces that dictated cost cutting was explained. The new task sequence and piecework rate were "thoroughly" explained by the time study engineer, questions were answered and the ladies sent to their stations to begin implementing the required changes. The usual "change bonus" was immediately put into effect for all. This would compensate for piece work earnings that would be lost while workers relearned their task routine and worked toward achieving a full standard of work output and piecework pay.

Experimental groups were also called to a group meeting. Workers were presented with two identical garments manufactured a year earlier and currently. The identical pajama produced a year prior had sold for twice the price the current product could demand. Harwood needed at least a 50% cut in its cost of the garment to stay competitive. With the foundation of need for cost reduction demonstrated, the group was challenged to find savings by cutting "frills and fancy work". Researchers reported that there was "general agreement" among workers that the goal of making the needed changes could be met. Management then laid out the process whereby the task would be redesigned and the piecework rate revised.

First, a time check study would be done on the task as presently performed. This served as a base-line check of prevailing standards and rates. Next, the "time study man" met with members of the group to solicit suggestions for elimination of unnecessary work. In the larger experimental group delegates who would participate in job redesign were chosen by operators. All members of the two smaller groups participated. Once they had identified opportunities for task revision, participants were trained in performance of the new job. Once trained, those who were delegates from the larger group introduced remaining members of their work group to the redesigned task. The new task design and piece work standards then were put into effect.

Differences between control and experimental groups were immediately clear and significant. The control group's output dropped to 75% of standard and remained at that level over the next three weeks, probably by tacit agreement within the group as protest to the change. Researchers reported "marked expressions of aggression against management", "conflict with the methods engineer", and "hostility against the supervisor". Grievances were filed through the union representative and two members of this group quit their jobs. A clear outpouring of negative sentiment followed the introduction of these work changes to the control group.

Work output of the three experimental groups initially dropped slightly for several days, and then rebounded upward. Groups two and three where all operators had participated in the work redesign reached the set production standard within three days of its implementation and their performance continued to rise, reaching 120% of standard within the first 14 days. Experimental group 1, represented by delegates in the redesign process, rose more gradually hitting the production standard on the fourteenth day then continuing to rise toward the higher than standard level achieved by the other two experimental groups. Throughout this time workers in all three experimental groups were cooperative and were said to have "worked well with the methods engineer, the training staff and the supervisor." There were no quits or grievances from anyone in these work groups.

A follow-on experiment was subsequently done with members of the original control group who were still on the payroll. When production had failed to return to standard after 32 days, this group was broken up and reassigned to other jobs.

Three and a half months later it was reassembled to work at a task comparable to that which they performed as the control group. The participative design earlier employed with the three experimental groups was applied to the reconstituted control group. Results in terms of achieving the revised standards and level of cooperation with representatives of management were consistent with those of the three experimental groups. Change was now comfortably accommodated and standards quickly met.

Coch and French's report of success with worker participation at the Harwood garment factory was timed to catch the attention of the new generation of social psychologists coming out of college with degrees financed by the World War II GI bill. It fueled the ideological push for greater worker participation in all kinds and levels of work and it spawned the community of research that has since produced a substantial body of research not only on worker participation but also on job satisfaction and worker commitment. The research findings that came out of the Harwood experience seemed to confirm that participation could be a useful lever for creating a more productive workplace. That was not a fully justifiable conclusion. Deficiencies in definition of participation as well as failure to specify what influence job satisfaction and commitment might have had in making participation work have made it difficult to explain how participation does its work. Fuller interpretation of the Coch and French research project must begin with more precise definitions of all three factors, participation, job satisfaction and commitment.

Commitment and job satisfaction both are emotion laden sentiments that should be capable of driving productivity either jointly or separately. Explanations as to how the two might work together to motivate productivity have unfortunately not been consistent. Some researchers have proposed that job satisfaction is the cause of work commitment, others that work commitment produces job satisfaction. Empirical studies designed to test these counter assumptions of causality have not offered evidence for either proposition. Instead, the better argument is that these factors are largely independent of one another, each with its own behavioral sources and purposes. They are substantially different personal sentiments derived of workers' experiences on the job, each operating in its own way.[6]

Commitment and job satisfaction are, indeed, different in important ways. Job satisfaction arises mostly from variations in working conditions. These include things like preferred quality of supervision, good pay and benefits, close match to personal preference for job design, the quality of relationships with co-workers, available opportunities for training and advancement, recognition for good work, or the needed tools and assistance required to perform the job. Job satisfaction can be defined by a summing up of these factors or by asking a global "overall satisfaction with the job" question. With both approaches job satisfaction is defined by working conditions.

Commitment is substantially different. Three distinctive qualities of commitment are recognized in the social science research literature. They are 1.) affective/emotional attachment, 2.) economic need for the job that produces persistence at it, and 3.) ideological sense of duty.

The first source, emotional attachment to the job, might possibly arise out of a high level of job satisfaction. It could also come from habits of loyalty, ideological faith in the organization's purpose and objectives, or from the job's inherent social fulfillments. This is commitment based on positive desire to be and remain a part of the organization.

Commitment also may result from fundamental need to earn a living wage with a paycheck. This second source is commitment driven by need. The third quality of commitment is founded on a sense of obligation to the employer or to those to whom promises of faithful persistence have been made. This is dutiful commitment.

Of these three kinds, the only quality of commitment that is necessarily influenced by job satisfaction is the emotional attachment aroused by good relations with manager and co-workers. In matters of sentiment, high job satisfaction is like high humidity in a dry forest; it reduces the likelihood that any conflagration will erupt. Commitment is analogous to the presence of trained fire fighters; it increases the chances of containing any outbreaks of dissatisfaction that occur. Good working conditions avert workplace problems and dissatisfaction; effective managers overcome those problems by nurturing worker commitment.[7]

The explanation offered by researchers that participation made the difference in worker cooperation in the change process fails to explain their results with clarity. With the foundation of more specific definitions in place, a fresh interpretation of the events in Marion, Virginia can perhaps be given to the Harwood story. Participation as involvement in decision making, had very little to do with the outcome. Workers did not necessarily expect or anticipate involvement in these decisions. Response of the control group to notice of change was not in the form of demand for greater participation. It was visceral rebuff of suddenly imposed change in their working conditions. Reaction of experimental groups was not satisfaction at participating, it was emotional response to the way the time study engineer introduced changes. In both instances, worker expectations for stable work continuity and pay were surprised. One approach got a very negative response, the other, a remarkably positive response.

Participation at Harwood involved multiple rudiments. First is that job satisfaction plummeted sharply in the control group when the new task design was introduced for immediate implementation using Harwood's prevailing method of change. Operators voiced their objections to disruption of their prevailing work conditions. Stable earnings and routines were about to be abruptly altered by the time study engineer who had redesigned their jobs to meet "competitive conditions". A rational, technical production decision was made by an outsider and imposed on the work group. Emotional upset was virtually guaranteed by the approach taken. Expectations for stable earnings and work processes were shattered. The internal cohesiveness of this intact working group is the second element invoked. It solidified workers' response into a shared goal of resisting change. They refused to meet the new production standard and vigorously resisted the same goal which was accepted without issue by operators in experimental groups. Any commitment based on economic need for the job was overcome by emotional bonding among control group workers. Workers in that group who felt no duty to anyone in maintaining their continued employment quit their jobs. Turnover increased as a result of job dissatisfaction.

The three experimental groups were surprised in a different way. First, they received a lesson in need for cost reductions required if the company was to compete, and, presumably, to provide them with continuing stable employment. This lesson was sufficiently straightforward to evoke such commitment as workers continued to have in keeping their jobs. Then operators were invited to offer suggestions to the time study engineer for elements of their task that could be altered or eliminated to reduce labor time. When they had done so, operators and the engineer settled on the trimmed down task design and tried it out. The new piecework rate was set from observation of workers trial performance. Through this approach members of the experimental groups had opportunity to take ownership of task revision and the piecework standard set for it. It was their work and their product.

Those operators in the larger experimental group who were not assisting in making revisions continued working under existing task design and standards as they adjusted emotionally to the prospect of change. Participants in the task redesign process, which included all members of experimental groups two and three, were paid to meet with the time study engineer and enjoyed the variety of participating in management level decisions about the redesign process. As they experienced this unexpected job variety, they had time to adjust to the coming change and, most importantly, to accept ownership of the new design and rates. Once set, the new design and rates were described by workers, according to researchers, as "our job" and "our rate", attitudes that would rule out group resistance to change. At the conclusion of the task redesign experience, those who had participated had moved from whatever cynicism they may have started with into full commitment to changes. The quality of that commitment is evident in the swiftness with which the smaller experimental groups, where all operators had participated, met and exceeded full standard production. The return of delegates to retrain members of the larger group put internal cohesiveness to work to bring non-participants into acceptance of the new standards rather than to resist them. Job dissatisfaction was avoided, commitment to continuing their jobs at Harwood was conserved and time to adjust emotionally to impending change inserted into the process. There was a cost to the employer, of course. While participating in job redesign and rate revision, workers were not making pajamas. Harwood sacrificed some production efficiency in return for acceptance of and commitment to the changes imposed. For that investment management gained significantly improved post-change-introduction job performance.

The emotional response of workers to the process itself determined the success with which change was implemented. An absolutely necessary component of that process, not acknowledged or described by the researchers was a radical shift in the role of the time study engineer away from that of technical decision maker. The engineer became a process mentor to the workers. It was a shift that was rediscovered in the 1960s and 1970s when Japanese manufacturers invented quality circles.[8] Quality circles took away responsibility for solving production line break-downs from industrial engineers as their exclusive province. With the support and assistance of engineers as mentors, workers designed their own solutions to production flow problems. Collaboration was introduced between those with intimate knowledge of the production process' workings and those with technical knowledge of production efficiency. That same collaboration earlier employed at Harwood accounted for how the process worked as it did.

The production engineer shifted from role of tormentor to role of mentor/advisor. The emotional tone of working relationship between technical expert and production operator was radically transformed.

Workers who are tormented become dissatisfied. Workers who are tormented as a group will resist as a unified group. Those who are supported in dealing with the potential of torment can become committed to adapting. Once commitment to job and manager has been restored or rebuilt, the productivity goals set for workers will be accepted. The skill and experience of the manager who recognizes and deals with these opportunities makes the difference. He/she knows what employees expect, like and dislike, and are committed to. Worker commitment is a precious resource. The skilled manager prizes and nourishes it.

As for participation, there never was or can be an all or none argument for it. Active worker involvement in making work place decisions is by no means the answer to all problems of commitment and job satisfaction.[9] There are several simple rules for application of participative management. Whenever a business decision has potential for defeating commitment by producing dissatisfaction, those it will affect should probably be included, maybe even asked to make it. Where there is cohesiveness in existing group identity, it becomes yet more critical. A united group can either block implementation by rebuffing the decision or, alternatively, support uncommitted members in embracing it. Full decision making participation, though, is rarely efficient. Where there is dissension within the group that could break into open conflict, the manager may need to assert authority to unilaterally impose a compromise decision. Where efficiency is imperative, the manager should make the decision and implement it promptly without wasting the time of others with needless debate. The role of manager in matters of participation is to judge the right course of action and guide the effort into the channel that works best. To participate or not to participate, is an open question. The manager's well-tempered judgment is all-critical to arriving at the best answer.

By contrast, there is no substitute for full worker commitment to decisions whether made participatively or imposed unilaterally. Commitment is the foundation of high productivity. Participation may sometimes be a means to establishing, repairing or restoring commitment. Job dissatisfaction becomes a problem only when it breaks out of tolerable boundaries and impairs prevailing commitment. Each, in perspective, has its role as contributor to sustaining productivity through application of the manager's craft.

8. HOW MUCH COMMITMENT GROWS ON THE MONEY TREE?

There can be no question about the motivational command of money. Money attracts, though not always optimally. The principal restraint on its attraction is the quality of activity required to attain a given monetary reward and the likelihood it will be dependably paid. A calculus of the personal pain, time commitment and self-gratification (or denigration) necessary to reach the payoff goes with every contest in pursuit of the cash. There are significant hurdles to overcome. The problem with money is that those who have it will part with it only grudgingly. That free lunch you heard about always has strings attached.

The object of monetary reward in an employment relationship is to secure the worker's commitment of time and effort toward production of specific goods or services. As long as that commitment is undiminished, the pay check plus sound, experienced management practices will usually be enough to get full effort. With the inevitable blemishes that time inflicts, some commitment will fade. Disappointed expectations of multiple kinds will temper the original commitment of time and effort. The complaints of fellow workers or friends about pay, benefits, poor working conditions, boredom with and lack of interest in work will all take their toll on commitment. Individuals on their own and complicit with others will progressively work out a new calculus of a day's work for a day's pay. Supervision may either tacitly accept the level of output offered or look for a way to move beyond it. There are hazards and potential for failure in either approach for the manager who does not understand the limits of his/her power. Much of that power resides in experience and skill applied to exercise of the manager's craft.

Setting high goals may be enough to optimize the motivation of money. It should always be at the top of the action list. Including workers as participants in making and implementing decisions can be another useful productivity motivator. Restructuring the job to build more interest or responsibility into it can raise output too. Where it is available, the opportunity to directly relate pay to work output can clearly make a difference. Some form of pay made directly contingent on amount or quality of output can be one of the devices used to push through obstructive habit or resistance without harmful confrontation. Incentive pay, piecework, commission, or group bonus can be considered. Cash payment beyond base pay can sometimes be an effective motivator of increased output. Where quality can be maintained and standards regularly revised without blow-back from workers, a well-designed piecework pay plan can increase output by about as much as 30%. It is authoritatively estimated that this is about twice what an effective goal setting approach can achieve.[1]

Piecework is not all peaches and cream. Quality is the major downside to it. Output can easily be accelerated by sacrificing quality and accepting the sloppy work syndrome. Examples of chronic poor quality produced in response to pressure for high quantity are easy to find on any level. The most dramatic and instructive can be are observed on the larger stages. Automobile assembly lines of the 1950s and 1960s, for instance, were rife with quality problems brought on by prevailing operating policies and practices. Chief among them was the assumption that full return on capital investment in production machinery required they be run with uninterrupted application of labor. A stalled production line brought near panic response from workers and supervisors to restart flow before pressure from the suits in the front office erupted. Quick fixes that ignored or overlooked operations flaws were the norm. Alleys off the main production lines were filled with vehicles missing parts from a previous assembly station, waiting for rework. Monday production, widely advertised as the poorest quality of the week, was avoided by knowledgeable purchasers. Shoddy quality was accepted as inevitability.[2] Japanese auto manufacturers built a reputation for exceptional quality by rethinking the quality problem. Their revised assumption was that a defective production line must shut down as long as necessary to find the underlying problem and fix it. Poor quality was unacceptable on any terms.

Even national economic policy can downplay and ignore quality. Single minded pursuit of sheer quantity in output at the expense of quality almost surely accelerated the collapse of the Soviet Union. Quantity production targets, demanded by Moscow's powerful central planners was the enemy of quality across the entire economy. At its most extreme, poor quality of steel pipes and production equipment, critical material required by the nation's oil fields, had to be purchased and imported on the world market using limited foreign exchange. Oil had to be sold to produce oil, a patently non-productive practice.[3]

A companion challenge to a successful incentive pay system arises when piecework rates do not take learning and increased efficiency into account resulting in unrevised rates over an extended time. Even where quality is strictly controlled, the use of time standard rates to set piecework pay creates the problem of rate revision observed in the Harwood plant. Demand for reduced cost and labor content driven by competitive forces is a continuous threat to piecework pay rate stability. The pressure for rate revision is, indeed, never ending. From observation of more than a century of continuous productivity advances it is clear that there is always opportunity for further improvement in any production method or process. Every task, every product, every work routine, every machine, every material can be improved, performed better, handled more efficiently, made better use of in the next production run or customer encounter. This phenomenon is the ubiquitous learning curve, a central productivity issue that will be treated at more length in Part III

Operation of the learning curve is demonstrated every time anyone takes up a new task that is to be performed repetitively. Early repetitions from a near standing start on the learning curve will demonstrate obvious evidence of change. Cost advances achieved further along the learning curve will be harder to find but will nonetheless exist, typically measured in single percentage digits over a year. The product of consistent and small percent changes is demonstrated in the effects of monetary inflation on the value of money. That same march of change puts continuous pressure on piecework rates for revision. They must periodically be reviewed and adjusted to reflect learning not only by workers, but also to recognizer improvement in productivity introduced by non-labor factors like better machinery or materials.

Failure to make those adjustments can quickly drive up costs and reduce competitiveness of the product or service offering. Ten years of failure to adjust rates in a major electrical apparatus manufacturing operation brought this lesson home to its management team. Union resistance to rate changes and industry dominance in the product line combined to keep piecework rates unchanged for a decade. At the end of that period workers accomplished in about two hours the tasks that earlier had constituted a measured full day's work. The company's nearest competitor, which had paid a straight hourly rate over the same ten years, was now significantly under-pricing the piecework product. Failure to revise piecework rates had spiraled labor cost out of control rendering the product line non-competitive. The problem of cost creep is not necessarily unique to incentive pay plans. It can be found in any pay scheme. Knowing it is there may not always result in avoiding it. Over-caution and timidity must never be allowed to block opportunity for improved revision in pay rates whether they are piecework or day rate.

Despite the problems of rate revision there is sound evidence for the utility of incentive pay schemes as motivators of enhanced productivity. The typical improvement will be somewhere between 10% to 30%.[4] An increase in output of this magnitude likely reflects what could be available in the surplus energy and skill hidden in jobs. The level of improvement achieved will be influenced in some part by trust in management. There may always be some skepticism on the part of workers. It is not uncommon for work groups to tacitly set and enforce a modest upper limit to piecework output to discourage management interest in a rate revision. Thus, some measure of restricted upper limit to piecework output is typical, maybe normal, on average. Once attained, it can become the level at which a day's work for a day's pay is once more tacitly agreed on among workers and supervision. That can settle into mediocrity too. Involving, as it does, extra labor, skill and trouble to time study and revise piece work rates periodically, implementing an incentive scheme may not always be cost effective. There could be legitimate question as to the substance or continuation of an expected payoff. Implementation of piece work pay is a management judgment call of no small significance.

Some attempts at incentive pay have been wildly successful. Where the benefits of piecework can be aggressively pushed they may yield exceptional results. The most convincing and enduring demonstration of such success is the Lincoln Electric Company of Cleveland, Ohio, a hundred year old manufacturer of arc welding equipment. Celebrated in a popular Harvard Business School case, Lincoln Electric introduces business strategy students to the manifold benefits of power and profit sharing, suggesting to many of them that therein may be found the mother lode of industrial democracy's benefits.[5]

Founded in 1895, Lincoln electric adopted an early policy of strict piecework pay supported by an all pervasive policy of worker participation in production decision making that has continued in effect up to the present time. Workers are expected to meet or exceed very high production output levels linked to piecework standards. The piecework incentive is amplified by a rating system and annual earnings based bonus that can double total pay. Working conditions are described as Spartan. Top management works out of plain, unadorned offices. The open, egalitarian culture of the organization provides foundation for full communication and maximum trust among management and employees. Operating information is shared with workers through an employees' advisory committee. Costs are tightly controlled and quality is assured by a part registration process that permits every warranty claim to be directly traced to the worker who produced the offending defect. The Lincoln product is accepted world wide as the most competitively priced, highest quality arc welder on the market.

Lincoln employees are a special class. Turnover is very low, and new workers are selected with care by a high level management committee that looks for workers who will fit the company's high productivity culture. Although Lincoln Electric job applicants are typically eager, their enthusiasm for its work ethic can disappear when the work demands of the job are encountered. High commitment to the prevailing work ethic is demanded. Not everyone finds sufferable Lincoln's unyielding insistence on extraordinary product reliability, high quality and maximum output. Abandonment of the job in the first eighteen months of employment is not uncommon. Lincoln Electric's culture of maximum commitment to product quality and productivity fits only a select kind of worker ambition and temperament. In recent times that has become a limitation on its corporate expansion strategy. The exceptionalness of its culture has set limits on how big the company can grow and whether it can cross national borders.

Attempted export of Lincoln Electric's productivity culture to Europe revealed that there are real limitations on the extent that foreign business culture will accommodate it. Yielding to stockholders' expectations for increased profit and revenue growth, Lincoln Electric acquired and established European manufacturing operations in the 1990s. It was soon discovered that the Lincoln style of extended work hours up to 58 a week did not fit European workers' expectation for a thirty-five hour standard. The cultural divide was much more troublesome than expected, resulting in a full rethinking of its appropriateness beyond US borders. Lincoln is not your customary plain vanilla company. Its fit in a distinctive scheme of business practices is far outside the norm. While it stands as demonstration of potential for maximum earnings with maximum effort, it is also a measure of the uncommonness of that preference.

A variant on piecework pay for production can be found in group incentive bonus systems and Scanlan type gain sharing plans employed by a significant portion of Fortune 1000 companies. Because they are tied directly to cost and profitability these approaches avoid the problems of periodic piecework rate change. They also lack the direct measure of individual output and its clear link to pay that piecework offers. Unlike the Lincoln Electric system that has enjoyed a decades long run of steady sales and high profitability supported by its pay incentives, gain sharing pay-outs are likely to vary from year to year. Such unpredictability risks disappointment of worker expectations that can sow doubt and generate diminished worker confidence in the plan. Profit sharing systems may be easier to adopt and apply, but require intensive administrative surveillance and control if trust and acceptance from all involved are to be maintained. As attractive as incentive pay systems might appear, they are not always an easy answer to increased productivity.[6]

Maximum output for maximum pay is a niche system of work compensation that does not fit all circumstances. That, indeed, is the verdict for most if not all incentive pay systems. As with every form of pay, settling on what is a day's pay for a day's work is no easy task. The pragmatic manager must have a good sense of what works in order to choose among the various pay strategies for settling on effective pay incentives. An appreciation of the problems of pay as incentive begins with some empirical reality checks that describe how pay and increases actually do work as productivity incentives. University of California Industrial Psychologists Mason Haire and Edwin Ghiselli investigated how job performance and pay progress of corporate employees were related with a twenty-five year long study of pay practices published in 1967. They concluded that performance had limited or little influence on long term pay progress. For the great majority of workers, the starting pay upon entry into the job is the largest single determinant of the pay that will be received at any later point in time. A blend of personal negotiating skill and special market circumstances existing at time of job candidacy sets the platform from which pay will rise. The influence of job performance is inevitably limited as an influence on pay progress because periodic pay raises are largely rewards for endurance, longevity and seniority. Haire and Ghiselli found that factors largely unrelated to work performance dominate in shaping pay progress.[7]

This reality is widely overlooked because the major forces that drive rising wages go easily unnoticed. Nearly all pay increases are determined by inflationary creep combined with incremental advances in productivity across the economy. On the working level, an illusion of performance based pay can be produced by spreading a range of increases around the calculated mean wage advance, typically those calculated by the US Department of Labor and industry associations. If, as example, the calculated mean wage advance is 2.5%, the likely variation could be from zero to five percent. In this range, top increases are a symbolic "attaboy" (or girl), while those at the bottom serve as an unsubtle hint to plan for retirement or to search out another job. The harshness of these messages is not lost on workers and can easily disrupt whatever motivatión to be productive that remains. Indeed, it takes a genuinely skilled manager to get away with effecting a real spread of the pay increase range without creating problems. Most managers conservatively opt for a flat distribution at or near the mean. If there is any spread, it will be limited to taking money from someone who won't raise an alarm to apply as reward for someone more favored.

There are other good reasons for avoiding any kind of discrimination in the award of pay increases. Spreading the range of pay increases is not necessarily a sound policy on multiple grounds. A manager who is asked to rank employees by performance, a favored practice among human resource managers, will quickly discover that the ranking can change as a function of emerging crises or opportunities, or just passage of time. The middle of a ranked pack is hard to judge and subject to sudden shuffling. The center rarely remains stable from one ranking to another. Those at the outer extremes of the distribution are somewhat more consistent but can vary also. Assuming that all are equals for purposes of pay increases makes sense in other practical terms. Trying to recognize performance with pay increases invites accusation of favoritism. Where performance differentiation is desired, it may be best to divorce performance evaluation from pay action altogether. The obvious outliers on the distribution curve can be identified for "development", the top performers for advancement, the lesser producers for candid counseling, pay increases not withstanding.

A strictly targeted uniform percent pay increase is often favored for purposes of financial control. The Department of Labor's calculated percent of labor compensation creep is popular among business' cash managers because it is handy as a device for setting and controlling budgeted wage costs. Top management can instruct a comptroller or chief financial officer to impose the cost of living increase percent as an absolute ceiling and thereby put raise-disbursing managers in the bind of dealing with it. If increases are timed out over the spread of a year, the effective impact on wage costs can become half the percentage target. Rarely is any differentiation made between departments or divisions of an organization on the basis of contribution or performance. Only where independence of financial records insulates operations is that likely to happen. The opportunities for the raise-disbursing manager to recognize performance within these constraints are meager.

Just about all the ways in which rewards can be differentially assigned as incentives to productivity turn out to have far too much potential to produce job dissatisfaction and performance disruption to be attractive. Major changes in pay are best handled as special cases justified by the factors that argue for it. Typically, indeed, significant changes in pay level, those that approach 20% or more in a year, occur only when circumstances are extraordinary. The fear of having a valued employee lured away by a competitor's higher pay, exceptional negotiating skill of the recipient, or recognition of high productivity potential will be the most likely drivers of major pay adjustments.

This approach leaves the "pack", bunched up by preexisting wage levels and target increases, largely subject to external economic forces. It becomes very difficult to recognize above average productivity within these constraints. Amidst all these limitations on advance in level of compensation, though, there is one predictable constant. Those who endure in their job steadily continue to advance, however incrementally, year by year. Job performance gets, at best, a feeble nod, or at worst, is ignored.

The most likely result of these limitations on assignment and adjustment of worker pay is that, at best, mediocre productivity is supported and rewarded. Examples of average performance then serve to set the norm of worker productivity and establish the standard of a day's work for a day's pay. The manager who passively allows this process to prevail will bear the burden of managing mediocrity. The status quo of a day's work for a day's pay will prevail until the manager resists it. Some form of incentive pay system may be a way out of this dilemma, even if only temporarily. There is another possible solution. The working manager can master the methods used to determine market worth of jobs using government data to justify setting and adjusting pay rates against something other than the "average". He/she can master the economics of market based pay and use it to advantage.

BLS PAY DATA AND STATISTICS

Establishing the pay level of any job approaches science when large population wage surveys are used. The most accessible and comprehensive data is found on the internet within the Bureau of Labor Statistics data base. This source offers salary-by-occupation for 822 US occupations.[8] BLS data can be target screened for specific wage data down to state and region for any specific job within the occupational employment survey (OES) codes used by the Government. The available data is comprehensive, statistically detailed, though is always out of date by one to two years. The time lag problem can be solved by mathematically updating wage data using Consumer Price Index (CPI) codes from the same data base. The result will be a best estimate of current prevailing pay rates. The system is sufficiently user-friendly to permit exploration of pertinent occupational codes and geographic regions without ever leaving the BLS data site.

The BLS internet data base is an exceedingly complex site with a genuinely vast fund of data that can require ten or more steps to arrive at the targeted information. The search begins with www.bls.gov/data/ . This opens the Bureau of Labor Statistics home page. By selecting the major category Databases, Tables and Calculators by Subject, an extended menu of available statistics is brought up. To pursue pay data choose the category Employment and sub-category Annual & Other. The further sub-category of Employment and Wages from Occupational Employment Survey (OES) offers the choice of a multi-screen data search. This opens the Occupational Employment Statistics screen with four options. The most useful is likely to be Multiple occupations for one geographic area. Continuing to the next level of search brings up the choice of geographically summarized pay data by national, state or area within state. The most useful option here will likely be "metropolitan or non-metropolitan area". Choose the most appropriate area and select continue to bring up the list of the 822 standard occupational survey codes for which data is collected in that geographic area. The list will likely be edited to include only those categories on which there is available data. From the (likely to be) very lengthy list, select those jobs one at a time that are of interest and designate All Data Types as the preferred form of analysis. At the end of this lengthy search odyssey a table will appear that offers data summary including means, median, percentiles and other wage data for the selected OES code as of the last date on which it was complete and current. Selection of one of the Consumer Price Indexes under Inflation and Prices on the BLS database listing will provide the adjustment factor for wage data.

The BLS site offers the option of downloading data into EXCEL spreadsheet format for personal storage and extended analysis.

Once armed with data on jobs within his/her unit a manager is positioned to negotiate knowledgeably with the candidate and the compensation specialist, human resource manager who serves as gate-keeper for approval of pay decisions. BLS data offers a broad lens view of the compensation picture that permits a range of pay strategy arguments. One need not be constrained by an existing judgment of the proper wage. The range of pay suggested by BLS tenth and ninetieth percentiles of pay opens the door to argument for strategies that range from the modestly paid entry level candidate in need of training to fully a qualified one who will become a production leader.

It is at the point of hire or promotion that the working manager will likely have the greatest leverage for managing pay within his/her unit for purposes of motivating productivity and shaping worker expectations. Access of BLS pay data puts him/her in position to negotiate knowledgably with the organization's compensation gate-keepers. If alternative data from other sources is offered by the gate-keeper to challenge a wage position suggested by the manager, full sharing of that additional data becomes appropriate. This kind of interaction initiates participative decision making with the company's compensation decision maker that might otherwise be bypassed or withheld, opening the door to use of a fuller range of pay options and strategies as performance incentives. The manager who has become experienced with pay data can further develop sources of pay data by networking managers of comparable talent in other companies to exchange current pay data. Once the compensation management intelligence domain has been breached, a good local network of employers can enable the working manager to function as an independent compensation decision maker. To make best use of that opportunity it will be important to understand available compensation strategies.

The basic strategies are three. The most conservative is to pay calculated mean market rate with adjustment to account for level of experience or qualification somewhere between the 25th and 75th internal company or market wage percentiles. That will usually allow for about 20 % variation in pay rate from the mean either way, enough to look like a difference but not so great that it can leave a manager out on a limb if the choice turns out bad. Neither is it sufficient to allow subsequent catch-up in compensation for an emerging star performer. Some risk must be endured. Hewing close to the mean on all wage decisions will be the safest strategy where a team effort requires internal group equity. Working in this range is a relatively low risk approach to managing wages.

Setting pay at or near the high end of the market range, at or around the 90th percentile, can be justifiable when a new business initiative goes beyond present working core competence to demand lead quality skill and experience. Getting the sought-after candidate will require a clearly attractive starting wage. In these circumstances it is best to use competent consulting advice supported by a thorough evaluation of candidate reputation and credentials in evaluating candidates. Even then, the hazard of making a bad choice at premium cost is moderately high. The safest choice will always be someone already in a job and applying the needed capabilities. Credentials can then still be deceiving. This is a risky strategy with potential for superior performance payoff.

Pay on the high end of the market range for any reason, and especially with hiring-in pay, must always be supported by measurable high work goals specified at the outset. This is the equivalent of providing fully incentivized pay that starts ahead of performance rather than following it. Although offering high starting wage for standout talent will certainly attract those who want high pay, it will not necessarily assure that all are ready to perform for it. An exception to offering the top end of the market range without strict high performance expectations might be where a critical skill is in tight supply and market surveys have not yet caught up with the shortage. In such circumstances offering better than average working conditions and benefits could be a safer and less costly incentive.

High pay for high performance is always a risky strategy. Buying strong performance rarely works consistently. Aggressively recruited professional athletes offer ample evidence of the risks of pay before performance. The regularity with which the highest expectations are disappointed and low or moderate ones are far exceeded is testimony to the uncertainty of high pay as performance insurance. The work (or play) itself can be sufficient incentive to high performance, even without high pay. Dazzlers who know how to sell themselves when they know the stakes are high will always defeat the best estimates of their real value. Sleepers who exhibit no extraordinary potential can become dazzlers without the incentive of high pay.

Below average pay is a strategy that offers significantly less than market value pay in order to control cost. It may also invite mediocre job performance in return. The downside of pay below market standards is the ease with which the underpaid change jobs. The absence of continuity of labor in work performance will usually add cost in training required and quality of output. Used as standard practice, pay below market will attract those workers who are least motivated and least employable. As a policy applied to the entry level worker, it can turn an employer into the training department for its competitors. Good performers who know they are underpaid will stay current with the job market and move on once their skill is mastered. Sudden defection for better opportunity risks instability of ongoing work performance in critical jobs. On the other side of the equation, too much stability at low pay can equally become a low productivity and job satisfaction problem. This is a moderately risky compensation strategy that may encourage mediocrity.

Money is central to keeping organized economic effort directed and disciplined to productive purposes. Money, though, does not necessarily assure maintenance of commitment. As with most other central factors and forces that influence work motivation and productivity, it must be skillfully and judiciously used toward achievement of the manager's purposes. It is one of several management elements of the manager's craft that can be used to support high productivity when understood.

9. SOME NOTES ON THE POWER OF A CONVERSATION

Selection of workers for entry level industrial employment in the late nineteenth and early twentieth centuries was straightforward. A gang boss went to the hiring gate in the morning. At his appearance the crowd of hopefuls surged forward, the strongest at the front, the weaker, some in early stages of starvation, at the rear. The boss looked for those who appeared most healthy and eager, signaled them to come forward and ushered them into the plant. Once inside, the new worker either did as told and fitted into the crudely organized work process or was quickly found inept and fired. It was a mostly messy process of self-selection and self-training.

Engineered job structure introduced by Frederick Winslow Taylor 's orthodoxy of time studied work standards and Henry Ford's assembly line precision demanded greater orderliness. Efficiency in production organization and flow demanded efficiency in selection and placement. The recently invented test of general intelligence soon became the general purpose answer to employment candidate screening. Science applied to industrial management was matched with the science of human aptitude measurement.

Historically, the frequency and volume of psychological research studies concerned with prediction of job performance is second only to that of job satisfaction. Use of aptitude measures in job placement began several decades earlier than did job satisfaction research and was based on much larger subject populations, commonly in the thousands and more. During World War I almost one and three quarter million military recruits were administered the army alpha and beta intelligence tests for the purpose of screening out those deemed eugenically inferior. Later they were used to classify three and half million men into technical assignments and for placement in officer training. Aptitude testing for job placement thereupon entered the scene on a major scale in 1917 and 1918. In much more elaborate and refined form it continues as a central military practice to the present day.[1]

Widely viewed as the solution to more efficient use of human talent, testing for vocational placement proliferated through the 1920s. The earliest version of the Scholastic Aptitude Test was first administered to 8,000 college bound high school seniors in 1926. [2] Post World War II vocational testing and counseling was offered to tens of thousands of returning military veterans by the Veterans Administration. By mid-twentieth century, industrial psychologists were fully committed to prediction of job performance with intelligence and aptitude tests. By the 1970s hundreds of research articles were in print extolling the utility of aptitude tests for selection and placement of job candidates. Meta-analyses that followed established general intelligence as the single best overall predictor of job performance.

Similar to results with job satisfaction studies, these meta-analyses revealed that performance on general intelligence measures demonstrated only moderate correlations with productivity. Selection instruments, though, are measures of actual performance, not collections of self-report sentiments like job satisfaction. Thus the "scores" they yield can vary over an extended scale that represents differentiated abilities at multiple levels of performance. This invites opportunity to set a minimum cut-off score. In theory, only the "best" are selected when those below the acceptance threshold are eliminated from consideration. It is a selection method requires a very large pool of candidates and depends entirely on the mathematical odds of success. Some of those who meet the cut-off criteria turn out to be poor performers, some who fail it might have been successful. Selection based on predicted job performance discriminates among job candidates solely on the basis of objective test performance. By excluding all forms of human judgment, the process is rendered scientific but soulless. The most that can be said is that the using tests of general intelligence to predict job performance is a valid and objective way to somewhat improve personnel selection decisions. Because measurement based predictions are, at best, crude and imprecise, there is always question as to how justifiable their use may be.

Intelligence measures are demonstrably better at predicting success at training. Correlation of general intelligence with training outcomes is about twice as strong as that found for job performance. There is good rational to this. Training depends heavily on language skill for both trainer and trainee. The twentieth century introduced many new complex job sets that are more efficiently learned from a verbalized description of their steps than from merely observing and mimicking the actions of a mentor or trainer. Learning, even of dominantly manual routines, has been substantially intellectualized with detailed, accurate descriptions of the work process that can accelerate learning because they can be quickly communicated and understood. Intelligence measures used to select for training are cost effective. It makes perfect sense for almost every form of training program to use some kind of aptitude testing to qualify and select among candidates.[3]

Intelligence tests are also very good predictors of formal academic learning, so much so that they are often called tests of academic aptitude. Academic performance in the form of grades or grade point averages is commonly used as a surrogate for an intelligence test score in hiring. Educational credentials are high quality evidence of ability to use language to learn and adapt to social opportunities and requirements of all kinds. The power of those credentials lies in a demonstrated mastery of the language skills required to deal with intellectualized education, and the candidate's demonstrated commitment to an extended program of skill mastery. The high school diploma and university degree are confirmation of competent performance in a complex social structure -- the educational institution. They are a generally sufficient substitute for any form of IQ test, although many kinds of work that require technical knowledge may still merit specific aptitude pre-testing.

Basic level IQ testing used for pre-employment selection of high school and college graduates is unnecessary overkill. Any formal test of intellectual ability other than one of specific job related skill or aptitude is hard to justify. Objectifying the employment selection decision entirely on the basis of formal test performance offers only a beginning sketch of the individual as a unique human being. It is cold, impersonal and, to some, insulting. The entry process must not be a gauntlet to be run that tests patience, persistence or tolerance for mistreatment, either by design or through inadvertence. Neither should it raise expectations for a job without high standards. It must all be done with full regard for the candidate's personal space and pride. Testing and treating the candidate rudely in a manner that communicates mistrust or disrespect is not a foundation on which to begin a committed working relationship. The initial evaluative interview is especially critical because it can bruise and dispirit if done badly. The candidate who comes through evaluation and accepts the job feeling mauled will not quickly forget the cost. The pre-employment hurdles to be jumped must be reasonable and relevant. Once successfully negotiated, the new employee should feel comfortable and self-confident in the coming relationship.

Selection is a point where the manager has opportunity to shape attitudes and expectations in support of worker commitment and productivity. Securing and preserving productive commitment begins at hire with a sound strategy for defining the job to be done and specifying the capabilities needed to support performance. To maintain commitment over the longer range the manager must begin to know the person in sufficient depth to adjust job fit at the outset and throughout the succeeding employment relationship. Getting to know the job candidate to an extent that allows good estimates of future job performance is not just necessary, it is critical.

The practices that go into the selection decision should themselves be evaluated and implemented judiciously to assure they are appropriate and fair. The pre-employment process offers the candidate his/her initial impression of company culture. The message it conveys should not be inadvertent or unplanned. The pre-employment process is where the company culture and advantages of participation in it must be accurately portrayed. That description should be thoughtfully defined and coordinated between hiring manager and the supporting gate-keepers to entry employment.

QUALITIES OF TEMPERAMENT CLARIFIED

Assessment of knowledge and intellect alone leaves out a large part of the candidate's qualities as a worker, especially those that pertain to commitment and teamwork. It has long been recognized that personal attitude is at least as critical to good work performance as intelligence. Beyond the fundamentals of intellectual participation in complex organization, there is distinct merit in evaluating temperamental fit to the job and/or workplace environment. This is the realm of personality testing. Most early measures of personality were idiosyncratic to a particular researcher and his/her study design. Interpretation was rarely standardized or consistent. Despite the relative crudeness of these measures of personality, they were often shown to correlate with job success at near or about the same level as general intelligence. Differences in temperament can influence the quality of job performance. The question was, why and how?

The complexities of human personality and temperament that long resisted rational orderliness for predictive use, had to await the availability of modern computing power. Personality is not readily reduced to a numeric score of ability like intelligence. It is a quality of social behavior. In the 1960s, innovative social psychological research began to refine and categorize personality factors by examining the structure of their expression through language. The result was development of a widely shared academic consensus that culminated in general acceptance of the five factor model (FFM) of human personality.

Once common personality dimensions were identified and rationally established, job performance prediction could advance to another level. Personality instruments based on reliable measurement offered by the "big five" factors could be used as standard predictors of temperament. Quality of job performance began to be correlated with these five standardized personal qualities: openness to new experience, conscientiousness, outgoingness, cooperativeness and emotional stability. This opened opportunity for application of meta-analysis methodology on still another level of selection for jobs.[4]

The first and foremost finding that came out of this analytical effort is of central significance to the selection process. Worker conscientiousness was clearly established as the second most significant predictor of job success after general intelligence. Thus, of the five accepted personality factors, conscientiousness stands apart in importance. The science of selection firmly had established general intelligence as a reliable predictor of job success. That conclusion was now expanded to add another major predictor to the inner circle, the temperamental quality of conscientiousness. This factor is defined by qualities like self-discipline, dutifulness, persistence, orderliness, exactingness. These traits are foundational to commitment. The big five factor of conscientiousness might, indeed, be alternatively branded capacity for commitment.[5]

This is not to say that others of the big five personality traits are unimportant. All five factors of temperament are found to correlate with job performance in ways that are relevant to selection. Like most other correlations encountered in personnel research, all five, including conscientiousness, correlate significantly but only modestly. This is less an issue of concern with personality factors than with job satisfaction. Although personality-performance correlations are generally modest, there are good reasons for high confidence that they represent real sources of performance causality. Outside of statistical significance alone, the base of research evidence for that confidence rests on the very large populations on which findings are based. The size of the samples used in personality research assures that temperament factors are clearly independent of and relevant to all kinds of job performance.

There is strong logical argument for selection based on estimates of a candidate's temperament that takes confidence in them still further. Personality test scores and interview ratings are elastic yardsticks, subject to much error and inherently low in reliability. Hard measures of job performance against which to correlate personality factors are rare. Most gauges of work performance are subjective or indirect like supervisor ratings or self-reports. They, too, are of questionable reliability. Validating the correlation of temperament measures with equally crude measures of job performance must overcome considerable imprecision in all the measurements used. Inexact measures that are correlated with one another introduce high levels of error into correlative estimates. Significant correlation emerges in spite of these problems of measurement. Significant and relevant findings based on such imprecise measures across large populations and multiple studies speak to a strong underlying association because of their crudeness.[6]

Beyond methodological arguments for embracing the relevance of temperament factors to job selection is the intuitively impelling conviction that they ought to be of importance. Attitude must be a contributing factor to job performance despite the fact that the hows and whys are difficult to pin down. The relatively weak evidence of science is buttressed both by common sense and logical arguments in favor of temperament as a useful factor for evaluating and selecting job candidates.

On intuitive argument alone, capacity for commitment ought to be central to selection criteria. Commitment is fundamental to job performance. Conscientiousness as a job selection factor certainly ought to be significantly correlated with all kinds of tasks. Meta-analysis establishes convincingly that it is. Jobs from the level of semi-skilled up to professional, including managers, sales personnel and law enforcement were all included by one major meta-analysis. At every job level, conscientiousness was found relevant to job performance. How could it not be? Conscientiousness is fundamental to good work.

That does not say that selection of job candidates for highly conscientious temperaments is going to be easy. Those painful, self-disciplined, achievement focused behaviors that define conscientiousness are best demonstrated in the act of working itself. Confirmation of their possession as habits with a written personality questionnaire is always uncertain and to some extent unreliable on self-serving grounds. Candidates can be coached to appear conscientious. Attempted confirmation through reference checks is more often than not futile. Even observations on the job can be unreliable. People can differ widely in exhibited conscientiousness from time to time and circumstance to circumstance. For most jobs, moderate conscientiousness will do if it can be cultivated by good management. To maximize its potential for the job at hand a manager must get to know and assess potential for conscientiousness in every candidate. Time must be invested in knowing the person. Getting a firm handle on personal qualities requires a personal approach.

Even if all the other personality factors were not significant, it would be desirable to invest time in assessing the conscientiousness of every job candidate. Fortuitously, there is benefit to assessing all five dimensions of temperament. Not unexpectedly, all of the other four personality dimensions have their special relevance to selection and job success. How important, depends on the kind of job to be filled. There is plenty of intuitive argument to support acceptance of that relevance.

All temperament dimensions, outgoing, sociable, assertive, extraverted, as well as conscientious can contribute significantly to the job success of managers and sales personnel. Those who maintain and function within the social channels of work need the requisite qualities that make for social proficiency. A confident, competent social presence is needed to coordinate and control any kind of work activity. These are also qualities that have long been popularly associated with leadership personalities.

Jobs that require innovation and learning benefit significantly from openness to experience. People who are imaginative and curious are needed in a wide variety of interests and pursuits. Those jobs that require solution of difficult problems, innovation, discovery, continuous learning and adaptive performance can benefit substantially from this personal quality.

The personality trait of agreeableness has special relevance to work situations that require close and continuing teamwork, no less so than the dimensions of conscientiousness and outgoingness. Teamwork can be disrupted by a disagreeable, uncooperative or unreliable member. Teamwork productivity is enhanced where the temperaments of members are generally more agreeable, socially outgoing and cooperative. Emotional stability is also found to correlate with effective team work. Low levels of conflict and disagreement can be troublesome to team performance.[7]

The presence of emotional instability as a quality of temperament may contribute to some kinds of performance. A certain amount of anxiousness concerning quality of one's work can be appropriate to professionalized jobs that involve risk and personal safety. Though irritability or anxiety that is noticeable will probably be cause for non-selection or dismissal, edgy temperament could still be judged tolerable in an unusually conscientious worker. Compulsive perfectionists have a place in every business organization.

Qualities of temperament are products of culture. They are the software of character. The categories proposed by the widely accepted five factor model of personality (FFM) are as much artifacts of our language as they are observable behaviors. There are multiple disagreements among researchers as to the exact boundaries between factors, and there is inevitable overlap among them. It is, for instance, sometimes hard to know where outgoingness stops and agreeableness begins. To aid the reader in using the dimension in evaluation interviews, a simple table of definitions is provided here with suggestions for observable behaviors that can be used to define each personality factor.

Personality is clearly an issue of relevance in managing temperamental fit to most if not all jobs. Every job can benefit from high levels of conscientiousness and commitment. The limited work discipline of poorly committed workers, however they may be otherwise willing, must be compensated for by the labors of their direct manager. Major breakdown in focus of commitment will be costly. It has to be anticipated that the most self-disciplined, conscientious and committed workers will quickly find work in any job market. The hard job is finding enough of that quality to build and manage a fully committed workforce. Thus, every selection decision ought to include a full evaluation of worker capacity for commitment. When the question is put directly, every candidate will likely claim it. A variety of five factor personality survey questionnaires exist that could be routinely administered as part of the screening process. That is not necessarily recommended. Factors of temperament are complex and fluid. Answers to surveys can be coached and shaded to the situation. Some personality profiles are flat and languid, others are strong and vibrant. Getting to know an individual's quality of character requires more than ten or twenty minutes checking off a list of personality descriptors. Convincingly verifying a person's capacity for commitment is more fully and reliably achieved through an in-depth interview that illuminates all qualities and habits of temperament. That pursuit can justify a significant investment of any manager's face-time with the candidate. It calls for an ongoing conversation with every candidate and every employee that illuminates qualities of temperament as it builds a personal bond of mutual commitment between manager and worker. A purposeful conversation is the best kind of temperament survey.

Dimensions Of Worker Temperament

CONSCIENTIOUSNESS

Orderly, Disciplined, reliable achiever **Evidence:** Punctual, Time oriented Plans and schedules ahead Concern for impression offered, may be stiff Exacting with details	Spontaneous, impulsive, unpredictable **Evidence:** Limited sense of time and timing Takes events as they come Loose and relaxed under pressure Comfortable with rough approximations

OPENNESS TO EXPERIENCE

Inventive, curious, adventurous imaginative **Evidence:** Wide range of interests Interested in details of interview setting Asks specifics concerning the job Innovative approach to problems Seeks out challenge in work	Conventional, literal minded, cautious **Evidence:** Focused interests and activities Attentive to immediate priorities Accepts job description as offered Prefers conventional routine in work

OUTGOINGNESS

Outgoing, Sociable, Energetic,
   Enthusiastic :
Evidence:
Enjoys being and working with people
Meet strangers easily
Garrulous, talkative
Seeks out excitement and activity
	Introverted, Self-sufficient,
	   slow to socialize
	Evidence:
	Most comfortable working
	   and being alone
	Takes little notice of others around
	Quiet, talks mostly when engaged
	Rarely exhibits outward enthusiasm

AGREEABLENESS

Cooperative, considerate,
   friendly, generous.
Evidence:
Accepts others as they
   present themselves
Quick to agree for the sake
   of agreement
Concerned for the feelings of others
Quick to sympathize
	Skeptical, distrusting, cynical,
	disparaging.
	Evidence:
	Questions the motives of others
	Skeptical of others assertions
	Unconcerned about others'
	   hurt feelings
	Little reaction to problems of others

EMOTIONAL STABILITY

Steady under stress, calm,
   rarely upset or moody
	Reactive to stress, moody,
	   easily agitated, worrier

Carrying out a purposeful conversation that brings out the desired evaluative observations and assessments of temperament requires practice and full preparation. When preparing to meet and interview a job candidate, qualities of temperament that are demonstrably relevant should first be identified. Behaviors commonly seen in current successful job holders can be matched with the extremes of relevant dimensions and listed for reference during the interview. The object will be to listen for events and experiences that point to those behaviors and, when encountered, encourage their development in more depth. Descriptions of big five temperament factors polar extremes serve mostly to anchor their definition. The personalities of real people will be more shaded and complex because personality is complex and patterns can be variable. Some individuals will stand out as exemplars of a trait extreme. They will personify the trait. Others may be flexible, moving toward one or other extremity of a dimension. Some personalities are flat, exhibiting little strength in any direction. There will be challenges to identifying the personal qualities of many people. That is to be expected in getting acquainted with new folks.

CONDUCTING THE PURPOSEFUL CONVERSATION

All aspects of the manager's craft are strengthened and focused when applied within the context an open, personal, purposeful conversation. This should be modeled on the open-ended problem solving interview process invented by Fritz Roethlisberger as part of the Hawthorne plant studies. It can be approached as a mutual information exchange that encourages full self-presentation. By way of full disclosure, it must be pointed out that mastery of open ended interviewing may require a fair degree of openness to experience on the part of the interviewing manager. It can lead to unexpected results.

Job interviewing as conversation must never become superficial or reutilized. Done well, it is time consuming and challenging. Done badly it suggests indifference to high work standards. Examples of poor job interviews are easy to cite because they occur so often. At its worst the job interview can become a game of "gotcha". The candidate is asked to parry "zingers", that put him/her "on the spot" by demanding admission of critical behaviors. Questions like "what was your biggest failure on that job", "what is your worst personal habit", "have you ever gotten mad enough to really want to punch out anyone", "how do you handle unfair criticism" yield little of relevance and may be insulting. Such questions start from an assumption of personal negatives in the candidate's temperament that asks for rebuttal. If the response is a clever parry or if it suggests embarrassment, should it be concluded that significant defensiveness has been encountered, or is it a sign that there is something to hide? If admission of personal weakness is offered, what do you make of it? If the candidate admits a significant personality flaw, should it be interpreted as evidence of honesty or as simple naiveté" If the candidate plays the game skillfully and side-steps the issue, is that evidence of mature judgment and experience or of effective training by paid professionals? Cute questions establish little beyond presence or absence of intellectual quickness. They can shut down the flow of honestly offered information.

The purposeful conversation is hijacked by any kind of game playing. It is thwarted by mechanically tracking a formal structure. The interview as any kind of predetermined ritual is a waste of everyone's time. If the candidate thus interviewed is hired, the working relationship has begun on a foundation of consummate superficiality. The boss has established the right to exercise authority; the candidate has demonstrated ability to avoid the most gross attempts at embarrassment. Even though some degree of mutual respect may have emerged from the contest, capacity for commitment has been ignored. The conversation pursued for purposes of pre-selection evaluation is a time to become acquainted, perhaps among the best that will be offered. Using the occasion productively requires that formalities be dissolved to permit a mutually respectful, informative, purposeful conversation.

The most effective interview is a pleasant, purposeful conversation that is focused on the workplace. Its purpose is to get acquainted so that subsequent roles as boss and employee will be comfortable and productive. Once initiated, an open ended conversation can easily run on for an hour or two. The manager's job is to keep track of what has and has not been said. Brief or even detailed notes can be taken to stay on top of the conversation's course. When a vein of data has been well covered, another can be cued into discussion. The manager listens for what is emphasized and what seems to be avoided. As the conversation lengthens and the interviewee's comfort level rises, cues can focus on potentially sensitive matters. Comments and questions that reflect appreciation of information offered can move the conversation forward. "That must have been hard for you". "I realize that disagreements are sometimes unavoidable." "It is very interesting that you made that choice" (or conclusion, or action). Throughout the conversation, the manager's interest is only secondarily to confirm claims of job skill and qualification. It is primarily in knowing better the person. Education, prior experience, and proper use of specialized work vocabulary establish skill capability and general ability. If they don't emerge, that raises questions. The candidate's description of work style with others opens the door to personality issues. The content of the candidate's words are the key to knowing the person as an individual. Eliciting a free flow of those words is the art of purposeful conversation.

USEFUL QUESTIONING

To open the conversation the interviewing manager should introduce him/herself in enough detail to set the candidate at ease. The introduction can end with a general description of what the interviewer wants the candidate to talk about. The interview should not begin with specific questions of substance like "what is your present salary/wage rate?", "do you have a family?", "are you still employed?" An ambiguously general inquiry like "tell me all about yourself" may sound too much like the context for a counseling or therapeutic interview. The purpose of the interview is to specifically evaluate the job fit. Inquiries like these are not the best foundation on which to launch a conversation. It is also too early to probe with "why do you want to work here", or "why do you think you would be a good employee of" (this organization). All such beginnings risk stifling openness and candor by seeming overly impatient.

A better approach to launching the conversation is to outline the general scope of the discussion with bundled questions that point to a set of general topics. "Please talk about anything that you think would be helpful to me in knowing you and your capabilities better. Describe your education, why you chose your fields and courses, what were your best subjects, the teachers who made the strongest impression on you. Run me through your work history and detail for me your most notable work achievements. Tell me about your interests at work and off the job too. If you have preferences in co-workers and managers, bring those up. OK?" A less complicated way to start is to unbundle and announce that "I'd like to know as much as possible about the skills and capabilities you bring to the position of" (fill in the title). This is general enough to open the conversation. Once you have started, you can sit back to discover, or rediscover, the power of those open, unstructured interviews pioneered by Hawthorne plant managers.

The manager as interviewer should listen attentively and say only as much as necessary to keep the conversation going throughout. He/she will take note of what has or has not been mentioned from a bundled question, take note of what is emphasized and what is overlooked. There should be no hurry to fill in the blanks. The process should flow until it is appropriate to ask "what about" (fill in the subject). This should be in the form of a "don't overlook this issue" comment that will cue the subject and demonstrate that you have been listening to what has been said.

Sometimes the candidate will invite a cue by asking 'what were the other things?" You can smile and restate, even expand issues that are relevant. Conversations are naturally pulled forward by lots of smiles, along with plenty of garden variety encouragements in the form of "that's interesting", "go on, that's very relevant", "I appreciate that" , "that's very good". Nods, smiles, expressions of approval and appreciation are the fuel of a good conversation. They keep the conversation moving.

Using a bundled list inquiry sends two implicit messages. The interviewer wants to cover a lot of territory and it is going to take some time to do that. It says that there will be no verbal sparring over details and that when a lull in conversation occurs there is shared responsibility to fill it. If during the conversation, the candidate seems to stall, it can be quite effective to simply sit quietly and wait. Waiting will emphasize that the candidate is expected to go on talking after organizing his/her thoughts.

The object of a purposeful conversation is to keep the candidate/worker talking comfortably as the interviewer interjects and interferes as little as possible. As the process unfolds it is always appropriate to ask for extension or clarification of what is being offered. Good questions will occur just from listening. Inquiries based on the candidate's words demonstrate that you are listening and will suggest that extended answers are always appropriate.

Inexperienced interviewers and those who do not yet grasp the art of the purposeful conversation will always feel pressure to structure the exchange at first, just as the Hawthorne interviewers did. They start with stock questions that discourage spontaneity in responses. Given the opportunity to talk about themselves most people will do so at length. Too much control over the course of the conversation will block the flow and distort the product, just as excessive control over work can depress productivity.

The best preparation for the purposeful conversation is to list the skills or experience that are essential to the job, identify the qualities of temperament that will and will not offer a fit, make a list of the things already known about the person, and offer comment only to either encourage continuation or to change course. A brief summary of kinds of questions and assertions that are useful is offered here as a start to the conversational process.

The initial conversation with a new work colleague should never be put off or forgotten. On occasion, there may be no opportunity to have that pre-employment conversation. The worker is transferring internally, or the candidate is acceptable on experience alone. There will still be opportunities for the in-depth personal conversation to occur. The beginning or end of the first day on the new job can be seized for that purpose. Any early occasion when time and opportunity presents itself can be used. If not then accomplished, or never quite finished, the first sit-down performance appraisal is a fully appropriate time, especially so if problems of job fit are emerging. Sooner or later the opportunity for more conversation will present itself. It should eagerly be exploited.

The purposeful, work relevant conversation is impelling evidence of the manager's commitment to and interest in the worker. A show of interest in the person as an individual is one of the most effective ways to build commitment toward job and boss. If, in that process, skills, interests, or ambitions can be discovered that permit a manager to devise and maintain the very best individual job fit, then worker commitment and productivity will benefit still more. Securing and preserving the commitment of those within the manager's realm of influence is the foundation upon which high performance goals are pursued and achieved. A great many other skills and objectives are certainly necessary to get there, but without the commitment of the workers and doers, there is little chance of performance rising above mediocrity. Therein lies the manager's personal path to high performance.

Commitment is usually close at hand as long as it has not been overwhelmed by indifference. Certainly, there is the original commitment that newly hired people bring to their task. The right tools and working conditions must be made available to support commitment. Recognition of a worker's contribution makes the work more intrinsically gratifying and commitment firmer. Just and respectful treatment support committed performance. Assuring that expectations are not excessively raised or needlessly demolished steers a course that maintains satisfaction and commitment. All the qualities of a high-quality working environment need to be regularly assessed, examined and adjusted to fit each individual. The manager is central to delivery of the essentials that assure a comfortable job fit and secures each worker's commitment. Part of that delivery task is knowing and applying those production processes that are necessary for to achieve high quality output against high work standards and goals. That comes in Part III. Part of it is knowing the individual worker in enough depth to adjust work place demands and apply the right controls. Exercising the power of a purposeful conversation to secure and hold commitment should be high on the list of priorities of every manager.

Inquiry Styles For A Purposeful Conversation

BUNDLED GENERAL QUESTIONS - *Opens the start gate without cueing specifics.*

- Tell me all about your job, your responsibilities, who you work with, your boss' way of supervising, the most challenging assignments you've held, the training you've been exposed to, anything at all that might help me appreciate the experience you bring.

- Tell me all about your formal education and training, the schools you attended, the years you were full time, the approaches your teachers followed, as well as the kinds of skill and knowledge you gained.

BUNDLED SPECIFIC QUESTIONS - *when bundled general questions are evaded.*

- Who were your customer contacts, what products did you sell, were there specific sales incentives, which lines were your personal specialties?

- Which were your two best courses in college, how did you choose them, did you get from them what you were expecting, and what new interests did you develop from them?

- What kinds of software and equipment did you use, were there proficiency measures in their use, were you trained in use of anything special or unusual, and what new skills did you have to develop?

GENERAL QUESTIONS - *To follow up missed issues in bundled questions.*

- Tell me all about your personal interests and activities outside of work.

- What were the most significant growth opportunities in your career?

- What was the reasoning behind that decision?

CONNECT-UP QUESTIONS - *Demonstrates listening and expands issues of interest.*

- You said earlier that you seek out challenge in your work. Can you describe for me the situations where you have found that challenge and how you met it?

- Those co-workers you described who were hard to work with, can you describe how they behaved on the job?

ASSUMPTION BASED QUESTIONS/ASSERTIONS- *Indirect Probes along the way.*

- You must have been disappointed by your boss' decision.

- When that assignment ended, you must have been relieved it was over.

- I can see you are the kind of person who would be bothered by that kind of thing.

CLARIFYING QUESTIONS - *Expresses interest and encourages extended answers.*

- Why was that important to you?

- Why was that customer so upset?

- When did that happen?

PART III:

SUSTAINING
PRODUCTIVITY

10. SPECIALIZATION, QUALITY OF WORK LIFE AND THE LEARNING CURVE

From the earliest beginnings of economic theory in eighteenth century Europe, division of labor has been assigned credit for the largest part of productive efficiency. The English philosopher David Hume spoke to the inherent limits of the individual effort. Achieving economic advantage and security, he observed, was possible only through "partition of employments". Specialization was common for manufacturing labor in his time and continued to dominate manufacturing processes throughout the nineteenth and twentieth centuries. With fragmentation of work the worker is defined as a narrow specialist contributing robot-like to collective productivity. Personal limitation is the price of order and efficiency.

Specialization in organization of work occurs easily. Any group assembled without pre-selection for experience or ability will inventory and organize its capabilities for performance of an assigned task. Once requirements of that task are defined, a blend of self-selection and aptitude trials will allocate group members across the work to be done. Individual specialties will develop out of differences in strength, qualities of temperament and personal task preferences. Division of labor seems to spontaneously arise in every community of purpose.

The economic advantage obtained from division of labor was most famously articulated by the Scottish philosopher, Adam Smith. In his justly influential and insightful opus, The Wealth of Nations, published first in 1776, Smith commented in detail on the productive power of work specialization in the manufacture of common straight pins.[1] In Adam Smith's time metal pins were as essential to the seamstress' art as they are today. An emerging document-based commerce also used pins to fasten or bind papers together. A pin might be inserted as binder through a buckling of several sheets, or through a hole punched in a stack of paper. In

Smith's time a small shaft of pointed metal lent to multiple creative applications no less than it does today.

By Smith's reckoning of the pin manufacture process, as many as eighteen different specialties contributed to this eighteenth century process. His description of the "peculiar trades" that ensue from the division of pin manufacturing labor specifies at least seven of those trades. "One man draws out the wire, another straights it, a third cuts it, a fourth points it, a fifth grinds it at the top for receiving a head; to make the head requires two or three distinct operations; to put it on is a peculiar business, to whiten the pins is another; it is even a trade by itself to put them in the paper." The fundamental qualities that define specialists in these various pin making trades illustrate how the benefits of specialization are achieved.

Eighteenth century pin manufacturing specialties were simple acts. They included stoking a hot fire, softening metal, drawing wire into small diameter through simple dies, cutting the wire in segments, grinding the point and top, attaching the head, chemically coating the surface, and poking the pins into papers. These acts require simple manual skills; shaping molten metal, manipulating cutters, grinders, polishers and applying chemicals. Pin makers had to be tolerant of heat, have good hand and finger dexterity, possess sharp visual acuity, and endure minor discomfort of smoke, pin-pokes or noxious chemicals. Given some opportunity for self-selection in such circumstances, most individuals found their specialty. They applied the skills and tolerances they possessed to making a living. As they did so, they committed to advancing their skill, mastering the characteristics of their materials and building their tolerances to the ambient stresses and environmental conditions encountered. They gained speed and efficiency of performance and expanded their contribution to economic advantage and security. Thereby did division of labor contribute to the greater good through the production of useful commodities much as it continues to do today.

Specialization, Quality Of Work Life And The Learning Curve

One's specialty establishes the individual's place in the larger social structure. The economic roles we play go a long way toward determining who we are as social players. The various specialties offered by the workplace confer social status and personal identity in ways that go well beyond the job. They assign economic reward and shape social outlook. Unfulfilled ability and ambition must either find other channels of productivity or shrivel in disuse. Narrow labor specialization inevitably wastes some human productive potential.

For the craft of managing to achieve fullest productivity, it must assess unapplied worker potential and encourage workers to break out of established job boundaries. That is not an unreasonable expectation. Over the long span of time, jobs inevitably evolve. Most of that evolution is of a revolutionary quality, it is produced by competitive crisis or entrepreneurial innovation that punctuates a long period of relative stability. Incremental evolution of work roles is not impossible, it is just very hard to achieve and manage. Organizations resist change by their nature. The manager who responds to worker potential by enriching or enlarging the job disrupts prevailing order. One change begets many others. There will be blow-back.

Within the prevailing schema of work specialization as a central lever on prosperity, the craft of managing emerged in Adam Smith's time as the coordinating agent of fragmented work. Fitting available talent to existing jobs is a fundamental part of the manager's job. Evaluation of that fit includes assessment of the candidate's performance skill and workplace tolerances. The conventional job fit necessarily excludes irrelevant capabilities and interests. For most of the history of the industrial revolution, that has meant exclusion of the worker's personal productive initiative. The worker is a worker, the manager manages.

Specialization that leaves out personal accountability is unlikely to sustain commitment to productivity. It more likely assures the emergence of boredom and disinterest that holds effort to the level of mediocrity. In seeking to improve individual commitment with a specialty, the need for periodic job redesign is too easily ignored by employers. Instead, pleasant distractions from the job routine are offered like child care facilities, physical fitness clubs, health fairs, weight loss programs and similar feel-good campaigns that serve to gloss over the lack of meaning, variety and autonomy in a job. Specialization gains productive efficiency and simplifies administrative priorities by ignoring the uniqueness and potential of individuals. Commitment and productivity suffer.

After a long course of evolution in narrow work specialties, widespread protest against meaningless work has come out in the latter half of the twentieth century. The 1960s decade of social turmoil saw emergence of the Quality of Work Life Movement as expression of that protest. Shallow job design that lacked meaning or purpose became the straw man of campaigns for major transformation in the work place. Narrow specialization began to be abandoned and emphasis shifted toward design of more interesting jobs. Legislation was introduced in the US Congress (though never enacted) calculated to remedy the problem of worker alienation in the American workplace. Narrow worker specialization came under aggressive assault.

Economic efficiency nevertheless continues to require specialization in work. The individual's work role is only a little less limited now than in David Hume's time. What has changed is the quality and mix of individual capabilities that must be specified in the job description. Jobs have become broader and more responsible. Workers must be more capable and committed. Work roles expand and improve in variety. Jobs are enhanced by becoming more meaningful, enriched, or enlarged. Specialization has not gone away; it has merely ratcheted up several levels of complexity.

High managerial productivity begins with fresh emphasis on job design that does not just evaluate the fit of seekers to jobs. It shapes jobs to fit the available labor pool and even to individuals.

Specialization, Quality Of Work Life And The Learning Curve

The manager does not just place round pegs into round holes. He/she observes the shape and quality of pegs and sometimes adjusts the available holes. That requires serious effort to achieve productive change through applying the methods of job enrichment, job enlargement, and job redesign. These are useful, standard techniques that first bubbled up into the management vocabulary out of the post World War II quality of work life movement. Each is a different kind and quality of approach to job enhancement that deserves clear definition. As a set of constructs they offer clarity to the manager's work as a job evolution engineer.[2]

Job enrichment is specialization invested with worker interest and purpose. Interest may be enhanced by allowing the worker access to information about market demand, customer needs, pricing constraints, customer quality complaints or real competitive threats. The worker is enlisted as participant in the solution of problems of product or service quality, pricing and delivery. Thereby he/she becomes involved with issues of production management and market position preservation. Enrichment does not come without cost. It requires commitment of production time to training and communication. Once initiated, information must be regularly updated and re-communicated. Job enrichment requires a change in the larger work culture that can involve significant up-front investment.

Job enlargement introduces work variety. Task simplicity is sacrificed for task diversity. Sequential or structurally related tasks are combined. An individual may be rotated through different tasks where changes are introduced in materials, tools, and products involved. Job enlargement can include added quality inspection, record keeping, customer interaction or self-evaluation activities.

Job enlargement is not without its problems. Too much enlargement may create overload that impairs performance. It can add skill requirements that make it harder to find a qualified replacement for the enlarged job. Adding significant responsibility without an adjustment in title or wages can create job dissatisfaction.

Enlargement that involves increased responsibility is often followed by complaints of insufficient pay. Job rotation with adequate training, though, can create a flexible work force that more quickly responds to changing product or service demand. A broadly multi-skilled employee can be a significant asset in a competitive market who is worthy of an added pay increment.

Job redesign may involve simplification of complex tasks, may upgrade the challenge in over-simplified work, or may introduce new tools, methods or processes into the work process. In its most adaptive form, the job may be redesigned to fit the special capabilities of the individual worker. At this level of work life enhancement, the employee may design his/her own job. Job redesign is not all roses, though. It can be disruptive of prevailing organization by introducing a ripple effect that requires changes in the work roles of others. This offers the possibility of added complexity and unexpected confusion in the manager's job.

Job enrichment, enlargement and redesign are big, crudely defined ideas. They are rarely implemented on anything more than an experimental or demonstration scale. If they were to be taken seriously, production processes would be in continuous flux. The work of a manager would involve continuous experiment with work and process design. Organizations exist to assure predictable, stable performance. Generating change in job structure risks error or breakdown of the existing work routine. Job descriptions must be revised. Pay rates may require modification. Relationships can be disrupted. The task of managing and coordinating work becomes more difficult. Why should anyone risk the problems that enhancement can create unless there is just no other choice?

For many jobs and industries the answer is that there is no other choice. The pace of technological and social change driven by continuous and unremitting competitive pressure within industries, across markets, between nations, all demand adaptive response. Clinging to established routine is the road to competitive failure. The manager's job is to meet challenges with adaptive changes. Big ideas like job enrichment, enlargement and redesign begin by enriching, enlarging and redesigning the manager's role. It is the manager who must bear the burden of the problems of job enhancement because it is not sufficient to merely accept a set of standardized jobs as the status quo. The people who occupy and perform highly specialized jobs need a manager who elicits their strongest commitment to productivity by offering them the most meaningful, intrinsically interesting, growth inducing work possible.

The Harwood manufacturing story demonstrates all three approaches to improving quality of work life. Job enrichment began with the simple object lesson of price change in the same product over the span of one year. Competition to maintain market share was creating pressure for change. This approach was not a mere management exhortation for greater cost efficiency. It was engagement of the workers in finding solution for a demonstrable problem of cost competition. Workers' jobs were enlarged when they were taken off the production line and asked to improve cost efficiency by identifying job elements that might be eliminated. This activity was mentored by the industrial engineer whose job was coincidentally redesigned to include duties as trainer and coach to these workers. Enlargement of workers' jobs required upgrading worker's skill as task designers. Redesign of the engineer's job was critical to gaining acceptance of change through their involvement. The result was radical redesign of the production organization at this level of work.

There was a much bigger lesson to be communicated by this result than just calling it worker participation. Researchers grossly under-interpreted the events of Harwood by adopting so ambiguous an interpretation. The work enhancement methods applied overcame worker rebuff and enlisted commitment. Change that overcomes likelihood of worker rebuff must be systemic. Change has to occur in key jobs that touch workers. Workers who are permitted to and instructed how to participate are capable of commitment. By permitting and instructing their participation

Harwood moved significantly ahead on the wave of industrial de-specialization. The larger US manufacturing industry might have earlier benefited from the discoveries job enrichment offers had they more clearly understood this lesson earlier.

Job enhancement can become revolutionary in scope. The extent to which enrichment, enlargement and redesign of work can be taken if pushed is demonstrated by team work production processes. I have observed a team of workers assembling a small electro-mechanical device, the postage meter. Each morning all the necessary parts and materials were delivered into the work area in sufficient quantity to support assembly of that day's goal for output. Most workers were able to perform all steps in the assembly process. As a team all began to assemble the base pieces of the product in the quantity needed for initiation of down-stream assembly. When sufficient first parts were ready, individuals peeled-off successively and moved to the next stage of assembly where they worked until enough parts were ready for the following stage, and so on through the day. At day's end, all the materials has been assembled and fabricated into a quality tested, finished product. As the work day concluded, the production area was fully cleared out. Meeting the production goal concluded the day's work.

In a standard assembly line process, each worker would have remained at his/her work station throughout the day, performing the same work routine until the line was shut down. At day's end, incomplete product would be left behind at vacant work stations until production resumed the next morning. With the team approach, each worker was cross-trained to perform assembly at multiple work stages. The group was self-paced as well as self-allocating of its time and skill across work hours and against the production goal. The foreman and an industrial engineer served as consultants to the team whenever problems arose. The team was collectively responsible for all stages of production. There was substantial enrichment and enlargement in play. Given the scope of responsibility, there was also potential to redesign of assembly and work flow processes. These workers had a sense of being producers, not just cogs in the production machine.

Team organization is not necessarily the answer to every need for job enrichment or enlargement. Teams require a commonality of purpose. A spirit of cooperation must prevail. The temperamental quality of agreeableness provides the lubricant for those frictions that inevitably arise out of closely coordinated team activity. Agreeableness is not necessarily a universal quality. Indeed, it can be a broader cultural issue. The cultural disposition of Americans toward rugged independence can suffocate agreement and defeat team activity. The use of group pay incentives or bonuses with teams may create resentment in those who feel they are carrying a disproportionate part of the work load. Teams are troublesome to manage when disagreement appears in them. Like the control group of workers at Harwood, teams can collude to suppress productivity when commitment to productivity is weak. Team production can be so totally threatening to employers who distrust employee collaboration that they will disrupt any emerging form of collective action, whether work related or personal.

Wherever teamwork is not workable or appropriate, designs for major enrichment or enlargement of individual jobs can still be developed and applied. Opportunity can be sought out for redesign of those jobs that reflect the special talent and capability of their incumbents. The manager who oversees the job that is to be expanded is at the center of the change process.

Jobs become fixed in their scope whenever organizational priority is focused on harmonized performance across related tasks. Fixed job descriptions simplify management of production flow. That may make them smoothly efficient, but not necessarily fully productive. The productive manager works toward greater flexibility in organizing. The analogue of a high productivity organization that flourishes with growth in jobs is the entrepreneurial company. Entrepreneurial leadership runs on leadership influence, shaping the organization as it grows, allowing productive talent to define the shape work. Jobs in an entrepreneurial business are constantly under revision to fit the capabilities of those performing them. Entrepreneurial companies surf the learning curve taking advantage of all the opportunities for change it offers.

The demands of a growing business do not permit needless waste of any available talent.

Entrepreneurial leaders run continually at the edge of full operating potential. High productivity managers operate in an entrepreneurial mode, pressing forward continually to enrich, enlarge and redesign jobs in their units. They recognize that the learning curve is always running. Ignoring or resisting its advance wastes opportunity for greater productivity, sets the stage for subsequent stagnation and mediocrity. The steeper the curve of learning, the more critical the pace and quality of job change. At the learning curve's slowest pace of discovery the illusion of stability opens the door to stagnation.

THE LEARNING CURVE

The Learning Curve is not just a common sense management idea; it is a fully developed process of cost estimation employed by industry bidders and government buyers to negotiate pricing of major equipment. It is a practice that became necessary with the technological escalation of material procurement following World War I.

The costing relevance of the learning curve was uncovered by the US Air Force Materiel Division in the 1920s. This division negotiated bids for construction of Army aircraft with the aircraft industry. Very large-ticket items like airplanes are typically ordered in limited batches of the same design. Production runs exhibit a distinctive pattern of cost decline. As experience with assembly is gained by the contractor, efficiency increases with each piece produced. It is not uncommon for labor cost of the fourth or fifth aircraft in the production queue to drop by 30% or more. Some learning from prior aircraft production may provide a faster start, but each production run is unique in its assembly labor patterns. Costs begin high and lessen over the total run. Costing the total production run of aircraft using the labor required for the first unit would grossly overestimate the cost of the entire production run. Costing for the last unit would penalize the shake down and learning phase of production.

The dilemma with limited batch costing is how to assure a fair price for the purchaser that offers a fair profit to the manufacturer. This issue was addressed by Theodore P. Wright in a 1936 technical monograph titled "Factors Affecting the Cost of Airplanes." With this publication the learning curve became public purchasing policy and a significant factor in the management of production labor cost for all time thereafter. All major equipment contracts for US military and NASA equipment have since been fashioned by sophisticated pricing practices based on the learning curve.

Simply stated, learning that involves a repetitive activity will show a constant percent improvement with every doubling of production quantity. The percent cost improvement from first to second will approximate that from second to fourth, from fourth to eighth, eighth to sixteenth and so on. At each doubling, cost will decline by about the same percentage. In principle, thus, the expected percent of learning improvement should be consistent across any doubling of output such as from tenth to twentieth, fiftieth to hundredth, one-hundred thousandth to two-hundred thousandth, five millionth to ten millionth. Estimates of real expected improvement based on military contract experience center around 20% improvement for each doubling, and range from 5% to 25% depending on product and type of labor involved. The learning curve phenomenon is sufficiently ubiquitous to be the foundation of an overall business strategy of many major corporations. There seems to be no limitation to its applicability and no avoiding it. It is applicable to just about any kind of work output.[3]

Robustness of the learning curve phenomenon is readily demonstrated by the continuous annual one to two percent improvement of economy wide labor cost that has been measured by the bureau of labor statistics over at least the past sixty years. Year by year, additional labor costs are shrunk out of US businesses products and services. Indeed, from observation of labor efficiencies achieved over the span of the entire industrial revolution, there is no reason to look for any end to productivity improvement. A continued progression of annually improved labor efficiencies is virtually a certainty. Learning goes on indefinitely.[4]

The experience curve represents a significant and easily overlooked lesson for managers; seeming stability of cost and efficiency with mature products and services is an illusion. Incremental improvement is always occurring and must not be ignored. The absolute minimum working estimate of labor cost reduction should be something like 1% to 2% annually. That has consequences for all forward budgeting and planning. If there is no reduction in labor cost, there should be a gradual rise in productivity. If productivity is not increased, there should be a long term cut in labor cost. The size of the increase or cut will depend on factors other than those that motivate productivity. Learning curve efficiencies are driven by experience, not by motivation. They must be anticipated and planned for.

The near universal tendency of managers at the working level to overlook or discount the learning curve accounts for the regularity with which corporate top management imposes arbitrary 10% or larger budget cuts on operating components. It is a crude but effective way to keep the business cost efficient. Unwillingness or failure to anticipate and manage the workings of the learning curve does not hold back the day of reckoning. At best it allows inefficiencies to accumulate until they must be faced. Facing that reckoning requires that improved tools, materials, methods, or processes be discovered that will re-energize the learning curve and raise productivity.

Specialization, Quality Of Work Life And The Learning Curve

Managers who ignore the ubiquity and stubborn persistence of the learning curve leave themselves and their workers at the mercy of other cost containment forces. The alternative is to look for, expect and support increased learning based productivity from every worker. Setting high goals for production is the simplest and surest lever for maintaining high productivity. Even if aggressively established, those goals will likely go stale and stall out it they are not regularly reinvigorated. Reducing cost by removing constraints on productivity can benefit from a variety of programmatic motivators. Recognition that the learning curve is always running provides the leverage to restarting or initiating cost reduction programs from time to time. Awards and recognitions can be conferred for demonstrable cost reductions. Separately negotiated goals for improvement of tools, processes, methods, materials use and personal skill are all potentially useful levers with which to drive those continuous advancements of productivity that are generated by learning and experience.

Specific goals for these improvements can appropriately be made part of any existing annual performance appraisal process. Performance appraisals are among the least favorable tasks of most managers. Their use as supporting documentation for periodic pay increases has made many appraisal discussions little more than an embarrassing apology for the limited increase awarded. Real criticism at appraisal time too often diminishes both worker motivation and productivity. It has long been recommended that a preferred practice is to separate pay issues from performance appraisals and focus uncritically on achievement of performance improvement goals in what should better be structured as a non-evaluative performance improvement discussion.[5] Managing the performance learning curve offers a constructive way to rehabilitate performance appraisals as a productive exchange between boss and worker.

The variety of ways that learning curve based cost improvement can be achieved offers diversity in the goals that individuals or teams can pursue. Different workers can be assigned different kinds of goals. One can be challenged to find ways to waste fewer materials, another to discover a better task sequence, yet someone else can be assigned to discover better tools. Formal skill training opportunities can be sought out for those individuals capable of benefiting from them. Customized goals and growth programs can be designed to fit each individual.

Failure to recognize and manage the learning curve is inexcusable. In the most candid terms possible, the learning curve is always a threat to long term work stability. That translates into a risk of job loss for those managers and workers who choose to ignore it. Comfortable complacency is hazardous to career security. Specialization may be fundamental to economic efficiency at all levels of organization, but specialties must evolve and change over time. There are no longer any specialties devoted to drawing and cutting wire for pins. The entire process is machine automated. The specialty that remains is that of machine tender. Wire pre-drawn on other machines in a different factory is loaded and threaded by the tender. The machine is adjusted and output of pins visually inspected for gross quality. Quality of each pin has been electronically inspected. Boxes of automatically papered pins are stacked for movement into storage. All of Adam Smith's eighteen workers have now been retrained to perform new trades.

Ethics and sound management practice require that every employee be encouraged and supported to grow out of their jobs into new ones. Like time and tide, the learning curve waits for no man - or woman. The rule is, adapt or join the unemployment line. Managers are no exception.

11. EFFICIENCY -- ENGINEERED TIME AND MOTION

Efficiency has a ring to it that just sounds positive. Anything that is efficient is fast, cost effective, good. The core of its technical meaning derives from the science of physics where the term describes the mathematical ratio of work performed to energy used. As applied to electricity used by an air conditioner, for instance, the number of cooling BTUs generated is measured and compared to the quantity of amps consumed over a fixed period of time. Two numbers are put into relationship as a ratio to describe efficiency.[1]

In wider usage the meaning of efficiency is frequently stretched, sometimes to the point of turning mechanical efficiency into a metaphor for anything that is positive, preferred or stylish. Computers are efficient if they respond to user input rapidly and store data compactly. Communications systems are efficient when they accept and transmit large inputs of messaging without failing. Markets are efficient when prices reflect available information. A business is efficient when expense is low and revenue high. Automobiles are efficient when they get high gas mileage.

Whether these examples are all real efficiencies in an energy use sense can be questioned. Fast computers and communications systems may gain speed at the expense of over-design that creates wasteful capacity utilization. Market information that offers exceptional price advantage may overwhelm with quantity of data. The best of it may be available to insiders only. Business expenses can be kept low by cutting costs to produce an inferior product or cheating workers and suppliers. Autos without air conditioning might be more gas efficient but a lot less comfortable. In the non-economic sphere of social relationships, there would be little interest in going to a birthday party said to be organized efficiently, and only a cynic would speak of having an efficient romance, much less any other kind of relationship. Some things should best be accepted as inefficient.

In the realm of business management, those things termed efficient may sometimes be cost effective, optimum, accomplished in the least amount of time, or least error prone. Trade-offs have to be made in achieving priorities. Critical judgments must be framed, best estimates calculated and some amount of sub-optimization of efficiency accepted. Efficiency is important, but it is not the only criterion of good managing.

At turn of the nineteenth century, efficiency was an unquestioned good. Over the forty year span from about 1890 to the onset of the Great Depression, elimination of waste and inefficiency was the universal answer to all problems of government and industry. Increased efficiency, in the eyes of progressives, required continuous advances in knowledge and education. Expanded university research departments, schools of business and engineering institutes were enthusiastically promoted as paths to social efficiency. Reform efficiencies were called for in the practice of medicine and education. Scientific research was pursued as the answer to every difficult social issue. Millionaires enthusiastically financed new research institutes dedicated to improved health, better education, more efficient government.[2]

This was the golden era of industrial efficiency and scientific management. Industrial efficiencies put forward in the methods and ideas of Frederick Winslow Taylor set the foundations for development of industrial engineering as the favored discipline of industrial efficiency seekers. Applied to Henry Ford's Model T assembly line these efficiencies revolutionized private transport. The Technocracy Movement of the 1930s proposed replacement of politicians by scientists and engineers. Its message was promoted through storefront reading rooms found in most major cities.[3] Efficiency was a moral imperative and the closest thing to a main stream political movement.

Worker specialization was first conjoined with efficiencies of production through blending the engineering methods of Frederick Winslow Taylor and the production innovations of

Henry Ford. Taylor, the engineer, pioneered time study method and disseminated his ideas widely through lectures and consulting in the late nineteenth century. Ford, the mechanic, adopted efficiently sequenced, time analyzed task specialization to meet demand for his wildly successful motor car. Assembly line technology blended with time analysis methods produced the first popularly affordable automobile and put the nation on wheels.[4]

Moving production line assembly of the Model T was born of pressing necessity. From its introduction in August of 1908, the Model T represented an engineering breakthrough. High quality chassis steel, improved engine and transmission design, easy, reliable operation on muddy, unpaved roads made it a superior choice for general purpose work and pleasure driving. Ford dealers sold cars as quickly as they received shipments and clamored for more. Earliest cars were assembled by teams of workers who crowded around it building up the assembly until finished and ready to roll away. As demand surged, this wasteful, labor intensive process threatened to exceed the labor supply. Demand doubled from 1910 to 1911, and then doubled again from 1911 to 1912. As production doubled, the work force doubled as well. Efficiency in assembly was imperative.

Ford and his key lieutenants consistently sought out the best materials, methods and tools to support production. Precision machine tools capable of producing interchangeable parts had already taken assembly beyond the stage of custom hand assembly. Improved engineering design and superior tooling invited still more advances in productivity. A breakthrough came with magneto assembly, the component that generated the combustion chamber spark. Each was assembled by a worker surrounded by parts at a bench. Time analysis from production records set an average individual assembly labor time at fifteen minutes. Sequential assembly was a possible answer to efficiencies needed.

Repositioned side by side along a waist high metal shelf, each man was given one or two parts install as the unit was pushed down the line on the shelf. Magneto assembly time on the sequential line immediately declined to thirteen minutes, ten seconds. Installation of a motorized conveyer belt gained an additional reduction. A time study analysis of each work station then evenly balanced assembly time down the line to permit steady, uninterrupted flow of production from beginning to end. Magnetos could now be assembled with five minutes of labor. Efficient work flow permitted one man to perform the work three had previously done.

A method that offered this much gain in efficiency could not be ignored. Engines and transmissions yielded next to moving conveyer belt production performed by worker specialists whose performance was exactingly directed by time study engineers. With the major production components of the Model T now produced by continuous assembly process, the last stage of efficiency implementation was inevitable. In the Summer of 1913, the final vehicle assembly line became the bottleneck to output goals. Magnetos, motors and transmissions were accumulating at the final assembly stage, waiting for that process to absorb them. The solution that had solved upstream production problems now made necessary its application at the end stage.

The first final assembly line positioned parts along an assembly corridor in sequence of installation. A rope attached to the chassis extended to a winch at the opposite end. As the winch dragged the chassis along the floor a crew of assemblers followed it, installing components as they went. Pre-winch line assembly time was calculated by time engineers at twelve and a half labor hours per car. Winch line assembly reduced that time by more than half. The result could not have been more impelling. In rapid succession, there appeared throughout the plant new conveyor belts, assembly lines and subassembly lines with parts suspended from moving overhead chains. By 1914 total labor time to build one Model T had shrunk to an hour and a half. The breakthrough engineered by Ford and his staff was not alone the car; it was the entire manufacturing process.

As the automobile industry was borning at the turn of the century, Frederick Taylor was preaching the gospel of time study efficiency to all who would hear it. Stop-watch analysis was already introducing standardized efficiencies into manufacturing processes well before Ford initiated his assembly system. By 1910, Taylorism, as some now called it, was fully abroad in Detroit and at the Ford assembly plant. Ford's engineers were equipped with stopwatches and trained in methods of industrial engineers. Time and motion analyses were fundamental to those efficiencies the moving assembly line offered. Stop-watches were production machines.[5]

Frederick Winslow Taylor's role as leading innovator of labor efficiency methods rested on a special combination of social and personal circumstance. His family lived in moderate luxury on income from properties it owned. Its daily routine was supported by the labors of a cook, maid and coachman. Young Frederick was expected to follow his lawyer dad into the practice of law. Socially Taylor was a product of his family's inherited wealth. Because personal issues blocked following the professional route set out for him, his career began as that of a wage laborer. It was a contradiction that could only be expected to shape his contribution to the practice of industrial management.

Mother Taylor rigorously home schooled son Frederick. In her role as teacher she enforced standards of hard work and discipline, qualities that would be his trademark as an industrialist. Enrolled in top college preparatory school Phillips Exeter Academy, Taylor was set on course to achieve his law degree at Harvard University. The rigor of Exeter's program was too much for his eyes. As consequence of his studies he developed severe eye strain that threatened blindness. Already accepted into his Harvard program, he withdrew from academic pursuits and sought an assignment as an apprentice pattern maker and machinist. His first job as a journeyman machinist was obtained through family connections at Midvale Steel Company of Philadelphia. Those connections and his level of education quickly took him upward into the ranks of

Midvale management. As could be expected, his perspective on work was that of the owner class. Taylor was a natural for the role of gang boss.

The late nineteenth century relationship of boss to worker that Taylor encountered was one of stalemate and inefficiency. Owners owned the machinery required for production. They offered the jobs and wrote the paychecks. Laborers performed work in dirty, unhealthy and often dangerous conditions that owners lacked the skill or willingness to perform. The bargain that established a fair day's wage was set by owners' satisfaction with sufficient profit and workers' ability to resist bosses' demands for more output. Put under too much pressure for production, they could cleverly disable machinery or spoil material, claiming breakdown from work overload. Bosses either accepted the excuse or fired the offender. They rarely had reliable knowledge as to how much output potential actually existed in machines capability or workers'skill. Periodic tries at motivating with piece work pay foundered whenever bosses saw increased output as evidence of concealed work capability and adjusted rates downward. In the end, bosses paid as much as necessary to keep the machinery manned with qualified workers. Workers did as much work as necessary to keep the bosses off their backs. Whenever bosses attempted to take control of production output, workers foiled their efforts. It was a stand-off.

Frederick Taylor had an advantage as a boss. He was trained to operate the machines and had worked as a machinist alongside his men. From observation and experience he knew that his fellow workers were slacking on their jobs. In his role as a fellow machinist he went along with the work group's restriction of production, but as boss he would not tolerate deliberate limitation of output. Frederick Taylor resolutely set about to bring discipline and efficiency to his shop. The year was approximately 1880.

Taylor's fight began with forthright announcement of his intentions. He set output standards that were to be compensated with a modified form of piecework pay. Workers who met the standards received an added increment of pay. To demonstrate that his standards were realistic, Taylor took over the lathe and demonstrated that they could be readily met. He discharged workers who fell below standards. Workers continued to balk and resist. He next hired and trained laborers who were eager to learn the machinist trade on condition that, once trained, they would agree to meet his output standard. When the new men broke their agreement and accepted the work group's output limit, Taylor cut their rate by half and dared them to earn it back by producing to standard. Workers complained to management and disabled machines in protest. Taylor announced that any worker whose machine broke would either pay part of the cost of repair or quit. Fines were levied and collected. Ultimately, workers capitulated and met the higher output standard. Stubborn persistence and tough disciplinary measures enabled Taylor to gain control of work standards despite the collusive practices of his workers.

The problem at root was inability of management to credibly argue what was a fair day's output. Taylor's hard won breakthrough was fragile and would likely not be sustained without clear standards and incentives. To that end, he set about every day to provide each worker with written instructions and an exact allowance of time for tasks assigned. Performance within the allotted time was rewarded with "extraordinary high wages", whereas failure merited only "ordinary wages". Disciplinary control was thereby established and a rudimentary piecework pay system installed to support steady achievement of Taylor's work output standards.

As the mix and complexity of work coming into the Midvale shop changed, Taylor was faced with the need for a more precise means of establishing time allowances on new work. Good labor estimates were well established for locomotive wheels and axles. Heavy ordnance was a bigger problem. He would use a stop watch. Midvale's successful bid on production of steel gun forgings for the Navy provided the beginnings of timed labor studies.

Intent on obtaining precise measures on which to base his labor time allowances Taylor took a stop watch onto the shop floor. To avoid influencing the pace of work if the worker became aware of timing, he initially concealed the instrument. His measures were crude. They did not yet break down the work into the discrete elements that could be analyzed and recombined for greater work efficiency. That would come later with the work of other industrial engineering pioneers. Taylor's concealed stop-watch timing of gun bore machine work on the shop floor was, nonetheless, the moment of birth for time and motion study.[6]

Word of Taylor's methods spread. Through a series of papers presented before the American Society of Mechanical Engineers in the 1990s he achieved wide exposure of his time study and piecework methods. Development of the methodology accelerated quickly, readying the emerging craft of industrial engineering to support development of assembly line technology.

Although the moving assembly line and time and motion analysis may seem simple practices, they can be quite complex. Each has down sides that can defeat efficiency. Applications and limitations must be understood to avoid the traps they offer. Both methods assume that wages are paid by units of time (hours) worked. Both are ways of organizing work so that labor cost is minimized, or at least controlled, and both have built in system rigidity that lends easily to breakdown if just about anything goes wrong.

An assembly line works by organizing in logical series a number of task specialists who perform their portion of work and hand it off to the next work station. At each work station, as the assigned task is completed and handed off, the next task arrives. In principle, the time allowed to complete the task at each station is exactly the same at every other station thereby assuring that there is no delay or interruption in the sequence of handoffs as the flow passes. If anything goes wrong, the entire flow can be stalled. Machine breakdown, bad parts, worker illness, will defeat continuous flow. A pile-up of work to be done will begin to form at the point of failure, eventually choking off the flow of work to all down-stream work stations. Letting incomplete jobs pass through keeps the line flowing but permits production of a defective product. At its worst, the entire process will break down in an attempt to keep the line running. Over-zealous pursuit of labor efficiency can be perverted into creation of a faulty, sub-standard product and spiral off into a major waste of labor time.

Chunking up the tasks on an assembly line into equivalent units of time is accomplished with time and motion analysis. A time study technician establishes the task time required for each job. At its most precise, each elemental motion is identified. Elements are accumulated and assigned time values from published tables. The end result is like the jobs designed at the Harwood plant. The smallest elements of the task are examined for savings in process time and a faster task design is created. The task, literally, is engineered for efficiencies.[7]

In more practical, less elaborate form, time to accomplish the task can be measured many times and the average used to set an output standard. In its crudest form, paid working hours are divided by counted units of output to establish a time standard. Using the best estimates or observations available, work stations are designed to be in balance with one another. To build up time at a station, tasks can be accumulated and assigned to a single worker. To break up larger task blocks, two or more workers are assigned to work simultaneously on the same task. Once the line is balanced, flow is continuous without delay or backup from beginning to end -- in theory at least.

Assembly line sequencing and time analysis can be applied in a general way to almost any kind of work. Document processing in a bank or government agency can be organized in sequential order and staffed using task time standards. Package handling on a shipping line or care of patients processed through an out-patient surgery center can be similarly task engineered using estimates from output records or time study specifications generated with stop watch analysis. Ultimately it is the manager of the operation who must make it all work. The most professionally done time study will contain some residual slack and eventually be rendered obsolete by advance on the learning curve. The best time analysis will quickly go out of date with product improvements. Task design can always be improved in some small way. Efficiency is a goal that, at best, is never more than temporarily achieved. Time studies and assembly lines can help.

FATIGUE, EFFICIENCY AND TIME AT WORK

Efficiency is about management of labor hours. The assembly line and time analysis are special strategies that address that purpose. In broader terms, good time management applies available compensated time with maximum effectiveness while avoiding idleness or blockages that waste time. Fatigue, energy, skill improvement and general satisfaction are left out of the efficiency equation as thus defined. Time as a resource well spent and well managed takes those factors into consideration.

Sequencing time-balanced tasks and setting output standards assumes that all workers experience time on the job in the same way. Much evidence is available to disprove that assumption. At the Hawthorne plant, response of test room workers to rest periods as well as to reduced work hours was an increase in work output. Over approximately two years, hours of work for the relay room women were reduced from 48 to just under 42 hours. Output per hour increased and weekly total did not fall. If time on the job is experienced in any uniform way these reductions in production time worked should have brought about a proportionate reduction in output. Instead, workers welcomed the changes enthusiastically and met management's expectation for undiminished output.

A research study of part-time "mothers" and "students" work shifts, prepared for General Electric's Corporate Employee Relations Department, took this conclusion still further. In the

1970s and 1980s reports of extraordinary productivity from part-timers were appearing in the Quality of Work Life literature. At one computer peripheral manufacturing plant in the Northwest US, a five hour "mothers" shift was generating daily output that came close to matching that of regular workers' full eight hour day. Part-timers working at a lesser hourly rate with no medical, vacation or retirement benefits were performing at embarrassingly high output rates. Attitude toward personally convenient work hours transformed part-timers' productive output. To some commentators, this was not so much a demonstration of good management as it was crass exploitation of a special labor source. Such discontinuities were too uncomfortable to be accepted. Mothers and students shifts afterward quietly disappeared or went covert.[8]

The disconnect between time worked and productivity demonstrated in these study reports had, in fact, much earlier been documented by Oxford don, H. M. Vernon. Vernon investigated work hours, fatigue and productivity during World War I for the British Industrial Fatigue Research Board. His report was published in 1921 under the title Industrial Fatigue and Efficiency. It drew heavily on actual records of World War I armaments production, and was an opportunity he described thus:

"The great war offered an unrivalled opportunity for obtaining the kind of information required, for vast numbers of men and women were engaged week after week, month after month, and even year after year, in making munitions... In the first eighteen months of the war it was the general custom to impose very long hours upon workers in order to obtain the biggest possible output, but it was gradually discovered that these long hours did not pay."[9]

War production offered a natural laboratory for study of the effects of reduced working time on work output. At the outset of war, heroically long working hours were typical in the manufacture of armaments. Across variety of laboring occupations, Vernon found that scaling back work weeks from seven days to six or less and cutting daily hours from 12 to 8 or less would produce an immediate drop in absolute output. Thereafter production gradually rose to match or exceed the original level, regardless of whether pay was piece work or day rate.

From analysis of detailed data on defense worker production, Vernon charted production when work weeks or hours were reduced. Output of female workers producing fuse bodies were studied over a continuous 93 week period. Sixty-six hours were worked during each of the first 24 weeks, followed by 28 weeks at 54.4 hours and a final 41 weeks at 47.5 hours. With the first change in work schedule unit worker output dropped then gradually rose until weekly output in period 2 matched that of period 1. With another reduction of hours in the third period, those levels were met and then exceeded. Working hours were reduced 28% and production rose by 13%. Reduction of women's hours from 65 to 48 per week on a different task where output was more limited by machinery resulted in loss of only 1% of the starting output rate. With a reduction of twenty-six percent in hours worked, output remained at 99% of that on longer hours.

Male workers sizing fuse bodies were studied over 22 consecutive months. When weekly hours were reduced from 66.7 to 60.2, production recovered to 105% of the first period level. A further reduction to 55.5 hours in the final term of observation saw production rise to 119% of the earlier production rate. The same results were found in other lines of work. When daily work shifts for tenders of open hearth steel furnaces were reduced from twelve to eight hours the usual initial drop in production occurred, then it gradually rose toward the former level. By the end of a year working a shorter eight hour shift the production of steel workers' was at 118% of the earlier twelve hour day level.

Vernon refers to this as an equilibrium effect wherein "short hours of quick work cause as much drain on physical energy as long hours of slow work." He concluded that recovery of output with reduced hours came about unconsciously because fatigue factors had been reduced. Though this may or may not be a sound explanation, something significant was clearly happening with workers observed by Vernon that challenged belief in output as an absolute function of time worked. Indeed, anyone who has worked long hours appreciates the drain that can occur in any lengthy, tedious job. It is an effect works both ways. Experienced operations managers operate on the assumption that the effect of overtime hours added to increase output will be short lived. In a matter of days, output will gradually fall back to the former pre-overtime level. They also know that short work week production can sometimes make up for time lost. Time as a measure of efficiency is so flexible that one might almost reasonably say it is elastic.

Skilled management can take advantage of that elasticity. In practice, there is nothing to prevent a manager from occasionally rewarding exceptional productivity by lopping off the last hours of an exceptional work day or work week. Implemented from time to time in an appropriately whimsical and unpredictable way, it could serve to reinforce (in Skinnerian behaviorist terms) the tendency to high productivity. There is, indeed, no legal constraint against paying for time not worked. That is exactly what payment for time on holidays and vacations is. The more likely constraint might be an over-zealous bookkeeper laboring under the conviction that time is money and pay claimed for non-worked hours is thievery.

Efficiency, it must be concluded, is not necessarily achieved solely through strict scheduling and application of available time. It can also be about health, well-being, personal attitude and overall quality of life. Ford and Taylor were clearly onto something with their efficiency improvement methods. Within constraints of the prevailing work culture and a fair day's work bargain, output can be increased through use of time studied; fragmented tasks that are cleverly sequenced for continuous work flow. But it is not entirely about time. Vernon's documentation makes it clear that time is not necessarily the ultimate constraint on efficient productivity.

The shift of manufacturing toward custom production and the rising domination of service industries complicate the manager's search for methods that assure efficiency. Ford's genius was solution of labor and machine capacity utilization issues with the assembly line. That requires demand for mass production. A different kind of genius is required to solve capacity issues with customized production and service offerings.

12. PRODUCTIVITY AND THE CAPACITY COST CRUNCH

Henry Ford's moving assembly line was a clever solution to multiple problems of efficiency. It directly lowered cost by reducing manpower needed. Engineered tasks reduced training time by using unskilled labor, the largest available and lowest wage cost pool. Performance time for simple, specialized tasks was standardized and balanced on the line for uninterrupted product flow. Labor was efficiently employed. Machinery was efficiently used. Sequenced work flow supported by engineered task design applied both labor and equipment at near maximum capacity -- IF; workers were not absent, machines did not break down, quality parts and components arrived on time, and market demand remained strong. Ford's assembly line worked wonderfully as long as tough management controls were applied, high worker commitment was maintained and there was mass market demand for a highly standardized product.

For two decades, from 1908 to 1928, Ford was master of the motor market with an auto design that remained rigidly fixed. Aftermarket modifications that improved the car's performance inevitably appeared. His engineering staff recognized the need for changes in design and recommended design improvements. Henry would hear none of it. Secret construction of an advanced prototype Model T was met with rejection so fierce that the vehicle had to be scrapped. Innovation was permitted only in production cost control methods.[1]

It could not last. Upstart manufacturer General Motors saw the readiness of the market for cars that were more stylish with more optional amenities. From Ford's one-auto-fits-all-needs product, the market began to fragment into style and price niches. Ford was overtaken by advance of the market. Newly developed materials, component designs, technology and tooling demanded that auto design be completely rethought. Ford too long pursued his inflexible, low cost strategy. Narrowly specialized, tightly engineered tasks worked marvelously while mass demand for the product continued. Ultimately, that demand disappeared and the market for the Model T collapsed. Forced into an engineering catch-up mode, Ford never quite caught up, at least not in that era.

Industrial progress has since replaced much of specialized labor with automated machinery that shrinks labor cost out of mass commodity production. Manufacturing labor content since has migrated into products and services that are custom or short run products. The dominant new industries focus on health, entertainment, communication, education, finance, insurance, government and sales where service is overriding. There may still be opportunity to engineer maximum efficiency into some services and short run manufactured products but the overall trend is toward flexible production. Worker skill as well as production tools and methods must be de-specialized. Efficiency must be redefined in terms of performance that is adaptive. Flexible job and machine design that supports market and customer demand for variety is the new norm. That imperative aside, the requirement for achieving the best available efficiencies in the performance of those flexible jobs has not been ruled out. Getting as much efficiency as possible means that, work must be managed to minimize the extent of inefficiencies that cannot otherwise be avoided.

Despite sea changes in the market, the basic business formula for achieving efficient use of labor and machinery remains fixed. Available machines and labor must be managed for cost effectiveness. Paid labor time must not be wasted needlessly. Return on investment from costly machinery and equipment requires they be used cost effectively. In economic terms, these are issues of capacity. The productive capacity of available labor, machinery and equipment must be pushed to the maximum possible without sacrificing quality or service. The cost effective modern manager must be an effective steward of labor and machine capacity.

High utilization of labor can be achieved with broadly trained, multi-skilled people who can be flexibly allocated to tasks as needed. High capacity utilization of equipment is achieved with general or multi-purpose machinery. The downside of labor and equipment flexibility is that there are limits to how much flexibility is practical. Cost trade-offs may be required. Some skills will be too highly paid or too rare to permit duplication. Some equipment may be so costly that excess capacity raises cost prohibitively. Excess capacity of these resources will be an offsetting cost drag. They must be used near full capacity. They are capacity constraints that must be tolerated without allowing them to become work flow bottlenecks. Interdependent work flow of any kind is vulnerable to wasted labor and machine time from bottlenecks in the flow sequence. The appearance of bottlenecks in any system of interdependent work flow squanders capacity and increases cost. Bottlenecks can wreck production schedules and waste capacity in the whole system. They are the largest source of inefficiency.

Bottlenecks abound in real life. For decades up to the 1990s, a bridge with only two lanes each way spanned the Connecticut river nearest its mouth. Though there were other routes to Boston and points north, it was still the best choice for travelers between New York City and Cape Cod, this despite it being a chronic bottleneck that regularly backed up weekend traffic for many miles. Local residents who needed to cross the bridge timed anticipated bottleneck backups carefully to either beat the crush or wait it out. Knowledgeable weekend vacationers traveled in the late night or earliest hours of the morning. This was an absolute capacity constraint that could be anticipated, but not overcome. Those who did not anticipate certain back-ups depleted many hours of their hoped for weekends trapped in stalled traffic.

The old Connecticut River bridge was a chronic bottleneck. It could be managed by choosing a less popular travel time. Other bottlenecks on this same route occurred by chance. In my commutes on Connecticut's lengthy stretch of I-95 I have at times encountered random bottlenecks in the form of accidents or road construction. Anticipation involved careful charting of alternative routes. I knew that in a traffic major shut-down the parallel stretch of Highway 1 would become the secondary bottleneck. I needed to locate the most direct back roads and calculate the lost time that their use would bring. Solving a bottleneck can mean working out the best of the bad alternatives. This is a close analogy to many common work flow bottlenecks in flexible production. They happen because of departure from the usual pattern of demand or an emergency.

Despite their ubiquity, bottlenecks are a management enigma. Much about managing capacity utilization is counter-intuitive. Consider these points:

- 100% utilization is not just a bottleneck, it is an absolute constraint that establishes the rate of all work flowing beyond it.

- Bottlenecks can emerge at points of capacity utilization of less than 50% if there is a sudden surge and capacity is wasted in scheduling.

- Capacity utilization in the range of 85% to 99% is an invitation to a bottleneck.

- Wasted (idle) capacity at work stations where expected utilization is high creates those bottlenecks.

- Once it emerges, every bottleneck is an absolute constraint to down stream flow until incoming flow dries it up.

- Preventing a point of high capacity utilization from becoming a bottleneck requires avoidance of idle capacity by quickly loading and keeping it loaded with work.

- Existence of a bottleneck at any point limits utilization at other points and can waste capacity throughout the system of flow.

- If every point of flow is at 100% capacity, there is no wasted capacity. That is the definition of a moving assembly line.[2]

The manager's job is to anticipate and prevent bottlenecks that waste capacity. Wrapping one's brain around these essential principles is no easy task. We'll give it a vigorous try here.

Bottlenecks can be either, chronic or random, parallel to the examples offered above. Chronic bottlenecks are built into the system. Once identified, they can be adjusted or anticipated. Random bottlenecks are a function of response to variable job and customer demand on the system. They come and go. Cost and schedule control requires that they be anticipated in advance so they can be fully utilized, avoided or worked around. The cost of chronic bottlenecks can be solved by accepting the limitations they put on work flow and cutting capacity at all other points of work flow. That is a variation on engineered work flow that makes it a problem of flow balance. It also becomes an absolute constraint on scheduling.

Random bottlenecks can often be managed with anticipatory planning and advance back-up plans. The kind of bottleneck that makes managers earn their salaries is one that is random, intermittent and can occur anywhere. This class of bottleneck occurs most often with custom short run product or service that does not allow standardized work flow. Variations in patterns of work flowing through the system introduce random capacity shortages and excesses. As soon as a bottleneck appears the system flow is blocked and becomes inefficient. Bottlenecks of this nature must be discovered or predicted and quickly loaded to maximize capacity usage in the system.

Businesses that accommodate variety in customer demand are always vulnerable to unexpected capacity overload. Hospital emergency rooms, automobile repair shops, income tax preparation services, machine shops, advertising and public relations firms and their like must all be prepared to handle a variety of differing customer needs at unpredictable times. Customized jobs create bumps and bulges in work flow. Any kind of variable work flow is thus open to appearance of bottlenecks. A surge in capacity usage can occur anywhere in the system at any time. To avoid stalling from overload, potential bottlenecks must be predicted. Managing an uncertain mix of work demands some kind of predictive simulation that estimates how flow will fill the system and where bottlenecks will likely develop.

Anticipation of bottlenecks begins with generating performance measures for those tasks that must be performed. Expected flow of work in-house is forecast and scrutinized for likely bottlenecks using best available task time estimates. That scrutiny may have to go beyond monthly, weekly or even daily analyses. A new projection of flow must sometimes be accomplished with every significant change in mix of work. The object of this forecasting is to identify potential bottlenecks so that they can be filled with work early to prevent capacity from being wasted at a critical point. Once identified, limited capacity must not be left idle. All other known or suspected points where limited capacity is likely must be also watched. If they are already used at or near capacity there is continuous risk that they will suddenly become overloaded.

Anticipating random bottlenecks for work that is in the system is not necessarily complicated. The minimum requirement is an estimate or measure of time required at each at each stage of flow. The total estimated working time is summed for each station for all jobs in the system that must pass that point. Beginning with the most heavily loaded stage, work is moved forward into it as rapidly as possible to load it early and keep it in use. The same is done with the next most heavily loaded stage and the next after that.

Precision in measurement for such estimates is rarely demanded. Estimates should best be conservatively set and lean toward the longest processing time that might be needed. Where estimates are weak, a trial run of the task on the work station can be timed on the clock. Existing production or accounting records that cover previous runs can be examined. Estimates of experienced operators can be averaged. Use of times and time estimates in this manner mimics time and motion study and engineered job analysis in broader, more practical ways. Discrete elements of hand motion may be useful in the design of labor intensive hand work. They are excess detail for purposes of designing an advertising program, organizing a banquet, reviewing contracts, or performing services in customers' homes. Simplified forecasting may focus the most important talent or costliest machinery in use. With time, the manager's personal experience with bottleneck encounters will further establish those most likely to occur. Good measures and records of process time will provide data for estimating the risk of appearance and avoidance of the bottleneck on another occasion.

Bottleneck management is good capacity utilization. It is a practical thing that should not require highly technical solutions. Some processes may be common enough to justify investment in computer simulation of work flow though it will rarely be cost effective to attempt creation of a computerized simulator for single run jobs. The measurement and anticipatory scrutiny processes outlined above are themselves a crude form of simulation that, ordinarily, should be sufficient.

Some general rules of thumb can be useful in managing with bottlenecks. When they occur at the beginning of the work flow a bottleneck will slow everything down afterward. Limited capacity at the head of production flow is no problem if down stream labor is adjusted to the amount of work flowing through the bottleneck. Inability to sustain sufficient flow to fill fixed down stream capacity can be costly though. The worst case I have seen involved unreliable automation technology at the head of labor intensive assembly and handling. The owner of the firm had bet on equipment that promised huge operating efficiencies. Almost daily breakdowns left workers downstream waiting for work. Once committed to this equipment, management had to keep workers waiting until the breakdown had been fixed. The offending equipment was inoperative as often as it was productive. If existing orders were to be filled at all, the gross inefficiency of this work flow had to be tolerated. The problem was never resolved and the business was ultimately bankrupted by the cost of this intolerable bottleneck at the head of work flow.

Bottlenecks embedded in the work flow can often be managed for full capacity use. For a fast start that minimizes capacity waste, jobs that require minimal work in front of the bottleneck should be put ahead of those with longer pre-bottleneck processing time. Jobs that require large amounts of time in the bottleneck should be accelerated to keep it working till others arrive. When the bottleneck is idle, capacity is lost. Failure to use all available bottleneck capacity wastes system capacity. Loading it early and heavily will increase capacity utilization and minimize cost.

Bottlenecks at the end of the flow may create scheduling problems but will seldom waste capacity upstream. To reduce cost, flow can be evened by reducing labor upstream. That does not solve schedule problems because bottlenecks at any point will obstruct meeting service time standards or product delivery schedules. When critical schedules cannot be met a decision must be made to either increase capacity at the bottleneck or negotiate more realistic schedules.[3]

DEALING WITH THE WHIMSICAL CUSTOMER

These general rules can help to improve capacity utilization. Some capacity issues, though, are of a more strategic nature. They demand explanation and resolution on a different level of management thinking. When customers come looking for service, in their own time and without appointment, capacity must exist that meets demand without exceeding customer tolerance for delay or disappointment. Banks, restaurants, retail stores, gas stations, walk-in medical clinics or emergency rooms, indeed, any kind of personal service offering, must have enough capacity to meet customer expectations. Too much excess can be costly, insufficiency can kill business.

Getting medical care is always bottlenecked by some form of restricted capacity. Walk-in clinics and emergency room services generally require hours of waiting by patients. Emergency room treatment is triaged according to urgency. Life threatening injury and heart complaints are usually accelerated for immediate handling. Sore throats and upset stomachs wait for hours. Counter-intuitively, though, 100% of capacity should not be the object of a well staffed emergency room. Incoming patients with serious complaints could die if all capability was loaded by earlier crises. Emergency room capacity will thus often be set at a level around 85%. Because demand is uneven, there will always be some unused capacity and there is still the possibility of waiting lines. The intuitive test for the right level of capacity will be the frequency with which capacity-in-use bumps up against 100% when crisis cases arrive.

At the other end of the capacity spectrum are real estate agents and jewelry store sales personnel. These are high margin sales with large commissions at stake. Such businesses will typically operate at 5% to 20% labor capacity. The intuitive test of an acceptable level of labor capacity here is the rarity of those occasions when a customer who looks like a buyer walks out before being served.

Between these outer boundaries of capacity management, the greater part of industries operate between 60% and 85%. This matches approximately the range of US industrial capacity percentages reported in statistical summaries of the Federal Reserve. Capacity in excess of 85% is generally regarded as unrealistic or impractical. Below 70% capacity utilization approaches unsustainable capacity waste. Similar limits will apply to most industries. Airlines, for instance, measure capacity in terms of seats filled. Operated at 85% capacity, their most popular flights will often operate close to or at full passenger load. At 60% capacity they will nearly always have empty seats on those same flights. Passenger trains, ski lifts, bridges and roadways, government offices, police and fire departments, package delivery services, banks, restaurants and supermarket checkout registers normally operate within that range. Businesses that attempt to stretch utilization percentages into nineties are courting performance gridlock. Those that fall to the 50s and below must be able to adjust pricing upward to compensate for reduced capacity use.

Very high or low percentage capacity utilization can become a means to gain strategic advantage. The earliest successes of the McDonald's fast food franchises were based literally on very rapid food preparation that kept hot hamburgers and fries available for service to customers within minutes after an order was placed. Success meeting the goal of near immediate service was measured by the percentage of food disposed of in the garbage because it had become cold. In similar fashion, convenience stores operate below capacity to attract customers who will tolerate no wait at the supermarket. They off-set low capacity use of labor with higher prices and limited stocks.

A pragmatic appreciation of capacity management comes with experience. Gaining that experience can take time and extract a cost. The unpredictable capacity requirements of a business startup or judgment of an inexperienced manager can be improved by using operations math. Best estimates of customer arrival at point of sale and likely length of time required to service each arrival can be entered into a simple equation to determine the approximate level of capacity required or available. Capacity can then be adjusted to achieve the balance of cost control and customer service that is desired.

This calculation can be kept simple for the math phobic manager. The critical estimate is percent capacity utilization. This estimate begins by selecting an appropriate frame of time over which to accumulate data. This may be an hour, day, week, month or any other convenient time span. Existing records of arrivals or an observed count the number of arriving customers can be used. Next, from samples of observed work the average length of time required to satisfy each customer's need is established. When the number of customers is multiplied by expected average service time, total expected productive time during the chosen time frame is calculated. The ratio of total time available in the analysis time frame to the total productive working time available yields the percent of expected capacity utilization.

Simple queuing equations will yield an estimate of the average waiting time in the work queue. Probabilities of longer and shorter queues can be estimated. The proper name for this method is queuing theory. Detailed technical descriptions of queuing theory as well as equations for calculation of waiting line lengths and times can be found on the internet with a search for waiting line equations.

Managing capacity is not necessarily rocket science. It can come intuitively with experience. The downside of intuition is that there may not be enough time to gain the experience needed to inform it. Experience with capacity management is cost critical for any business. Operations research theory can replace lack of capacity management experience when beginning from a cold start.

FINDING CAPACITY SOLUTIONS OUTSIDE THE BOX

The likely knee-jerk response to many emerging bottlenecks will be to schedule overtime. Overtime may sometimes solve the problem when used only as a brief surge of defensive response. Bottlenecks, though, can be stubborn. Once overtime is applied to the problem it may become chronic, eventually wasteful of still more capacity. A better solution may be to call in temporary or contract capacity to take the pressure off. Like most other solutions to an emerging capacity constraint, spare capacity will likely work better if thought through and planned in advance. An ingenious answer to finding excess capacity for a very tight capacity problem once presented itself in a small, high technology manufacturing operation.

This was a business driven by the imperative of unveiling each year a fresh product offering at a major national trade show. The electronics were assembled in-house, but very high quality plastic cases for the packaging had to be put out for contract. The bottleneck was design and construction of the steel dies used to mold these cases. Design of the case was done in-house by engineers under personal direction of the entrepreneur owner who revised and tweaked its specs right up to the moment of planned contract release. The design was then put out to a machine shop that had earlier contracted to construct the die on a very tight schedule. That schedule that usually required the contracting shop to put aside much work already in process and waste considerable of its own capacity handling the job entirely with in-house resources. There was high stress and risk at every step of meeting the die production schedule.

One shop approached the job of die fabrication with full confidence it could perform on time. The usual nervous back and forth of negotiation that seemed primed with preparatory excuses did not occur. This called for an explanation. How could this operation be so confident of their ability to perform? The answer was a stunner.

This large shop operated at near production capacity almost continuously. Only those parts of the job would be kept in-house for which more than sufficient machining capacity or flexibility was available. Capacity bottlenecks were anticipated and met by outsourcing to a network of smaller shops in a 200 mile geographic radius. Smaller shops were more flexible because much labor was done by an owner who was unconcerned about keeping normal work hours. Many small shops had high end automated equipment that was under-used. Unqualified to handle the entire job, a small shop could handle individual pieces of work. A good part of the contracting operations manager's job was to deliver outsourced work and pick it up on completion, sometimes going directly from one outsourcing shop to another.

This was a system that could work only because the contracting machine shop had much earlier tested the work capability of their networked shops and had confidence they could do the work right. The small, owner run shops were not as constrained by normal work schedules and sometimes worked straight through into the night or weekend to complete the work. They received a small premium rate for the work, the contracting shop took an override for managing the outsourcing, the schedule was met with time to spare.

Most of the lessons of time and capacity management are taught by this tale. There is potential for spare capacity all around waiting to be discovered and used. Once identified, contingency agreements can be worked out. Sources may be found that bring in retirees, independent contractors, or temporary agencies as capacity spare resources. A network of qualified moonlighters may have potential. The potential for relief of capacity constraints by these measures says that any occasion when a costly investment in equipment or talent to meet capacity needs is in play, use of independent contractors or part timers should be evaluated as an alternative possibility. Spare capacity that is qualified and on call can be a manager's career saver.

Rigid assumptions about time and working hours are challenged by the die machining story. The eight hour day, forty hour week with set hours need not be a straight-jacket on how work gets done. Labor need not be wasted waiting for work to flow down stream. Working hours can be offset and work begun when critical flow arrives. The mindset of an eight hour day can be replaced with awareness that there can be variation in length of work day within the forty hour week. It can be recognized that work weeks that get the job done on time can be less than forty hours. Assumptions about time that are set in policy stone may deserve challenge as likely capacity wasters. The manager who accepts them is donning his/her own straight jacket with too little complaint for that constraint. Timing can be made more flexible.

Capacity management is the foundation of cost control. It is easily overlooked or glossed over in favor of exhortations for attitude improvement and greater workforce participation in management decisions. The snarls that a critical bottleneck can create quickly render moot those issues. Working conditions must support high productivity. The best skill of a manager that is applied to controlling and committing workers is of no avail where capacity is poorly managed. High productivity demands all bases of productivity be touched.

13. BALANCED JUDGEMENT: RESULTS VS. RISK

Sustaining productivity is a balancing act. Cost must be controlled and quality maintained. Details must be mastered and priorities met. Results must be achieved without breaching laws, flaunting regulations or abandoning standards. Prudent risks must be undertaken and reasonable cautions observed. Responsibility must be shared and individual accountability maintained. Conventional organization structure offers support that reconciles some of these contradictory demands. That does not suborn bad choices. At crunch time, decisions are judged and appropriate rewards or penalties handed down.

Some security is found in the nature of organized effort. Functional departments tilt either toward following procedures or getting results. Technical disciplines specialize in orderly decision making. Engineers, accountants, routine medical practitioners, and lawyers pursue ordered careers bounded by procedures, rules, laws, accepted practices. Sales personnel repair and maintenance technicians, emergency response jobs and entrepreneurs, by contrast, set clear priorities and drive for results. Emphasis shifts from one context to the other. The manager who must fit only one of these contexts or the other may deem him/herself fortunate. The job has been simplified, or so it may seem. Complacency in the face of such simplicity can be a trap. The ability must be developed to judge those occasions when strict attention to detail is required against those where the right priority should be single-mindedly pursued. Whenever the job demands continuous juggling of priorities versus following rules or regulations, which is much of the time, the craft of managing is tested.

Most professions and industries are regulated in some fashion. Rules and regulations introduce complexity and the chance of civil or criminal charges when they are breached. The choice is between the highest profit and the least threat of legal or regulatory penalty. The decision making crunch that follows is severe and the blow-back from those regulated against the regulators is often defiant. Industries commit vast sums of money to the reduction of government regulatory clout. They actively lobby against added rules. Rules clearly interfere with getting results, but the rules never go away. One high visibility crisis is enough to impel stronger enforcement. At one time regulations are weakened, at another, strengthened. The working manager must build skill in working within the rules while never losing sight of results. The pursuit of results, though, can become an end in itself because results are so satisfying and profitable.

Achieving results is much about controlling cost and meeting schedules. In the operating manager's mode, this requires that strict priorities be set. Some risks are accepted that will be offset by results obtained. From the risk avoidance perspective, maintaining standards and containing risk is all about applying a disciplined work method that assures quality output, safe operation and a superior reputation. Quite different mind sets and tools are called for by the divergent purposes of avoiding risk and getting results.

Priorities arise from identification of high payoff outcomes. The conventional guide to discovering where those payoffs are to be found is the 80/20 rule. This is the common observation that in many circumstances, 80% of the value can be found in 20% of the contributing sources or events. Examples abound. Typically 80% of customer complaints are generated by 20% of products or services offered. Eighty percent of worker error is attributable to 20% of the work force. Eighty percent of cost is associated with 20% of materials or supplies. Eighty percent of sales come from 20% of products or services. Eighty percent of schedule delays are located in 20% of operating activities.

Dramatic short term improvement in customer complaints can be achieved by intensively focusing on those limited products or services that produced most past complaints. Fast, cost effective reduction in work errors can be obtained by retraining only those workers who have made the larger part of them. Significant reduction in cost of materials or supplies can be obtained with concentrated effort to negotiate lower prices, manage inventory more closely, or reduce waste in the most costly 20%. Revenue can be raised by focusing on only one key customer out of five. Schedules can be met by focusing on priority bottlenecks. Ruthlessly set priorities allow a manager to quickly and precisely go to the heart of most operating problems. This despite the probability, that pursuit of high payoff through priority setting will not necessarily go to the root of the problem. When one bad batch of materials, a single customer complaint, or a lone worker error can wipe out 80% of profits, chasing 80/20 priorities offers little comfort.

Managing risk, upholding the standard, protecting the brand name and assuring safety all require implanted work discipline and sound managerial judgment. Existence of any conceivable chance of disaster demands forethoughtful planning and training for the worst-case eventuality. Rules and regulations alone are not sufficient to fend off impending calamity. Neither is rational calculation of risk or statistical probability. In recent times, both have failed catastrophically.

The 1998 failure of Long Term Capital Management after Russia defaulted its bonds illustrates the folly of investing in the sure thing. Firm founders' status as Nobel laureates in economics offered no security when its highly leveraged house of cards began to fold. A decade later, little learning seemed to have been gleaned from the LTCM debacle when US financial markets teetered near collapse after the supposedly rock solid real estate market collapsed from internal financial rot. The soundness of risks that underlay these investment schemes was assured by exotic statistical analyses. Those analyses were not just flawed, they were other-worldly.

Statistics can mislead. Risk analysis based on statistical probability fails to account for the most improbable of catastrophic events. However unlikely a potential catastrophe may be in statistical terms, it cannot be ruled out by mathematics alone. The prudent manager is a worst case planner. Worst case crisis that is in any way plausible must be anticipated. Where life can be lost or the business wiped out a reliable monitoring process backed up with training and simulation of crisis response is good, sensible management practice. Time invested in practicing the Heimlich maneuver and cardiopulmonary resuscitation is a wise hedge against tragedy in many a health crisis.[1]

However prudent worst case planning may be, real time work priorities can become so much more urgent and impelling that worst case preparation looks like unaffordable waste of time. Priority management yields payoff in the near term. It earns recognition and reward for good managing. Penalties for failure to maintain standards, anticipate the outcome of risky activity or delivery of a shoddy product are somewhere out there in probabilistically distant space. They do not create the kind of focus that priorities command. The wrecked career or badly wounded business that may result from their sudden occurrence is too nasty to want to contemplate, especially so when the experts say they are highly improbable.

In the early spring of 2010 the semi-submersible oil drilling rig Deep Water Horizon was in the final stages of sealing off a well forty miles off the Louisiana shore in the Gulf of Mexico. Dynamically positioned by powerful diesel engines and stabilized on location with global positioning data, the Deep Water Horizon was attached to the head of an oil well located in the water almost a mile below. Operations on April 20th were in an accelerated mode that would bring the entire operation to a close by the end of that work shift. The drilling crew was on its final, twenty-first day of continuous daily twelve hour work shifts. Executives of BP, the well licensee, were on board to commend the crew for its work and see the conclusion of drilling operations. The Deep Water Horizon, an ocean going vessel with its own captain and crew, would soon move on to a new assignment on another ocean.

This well, the Macondo, had given drillers troubles from the beginning. The geological formation that held its oil riches was known for its porous and unstable character. Drilling mud, introduced into the well to hold back the pressure of oil and gas, could suddenly disappear into formation cracks, violently destabilizing the drilling floor. These "kicks" had more than once sent the drilling crew into full crisis recovery mode. Just six weeks earlier a particularly mean kick had left costly drilling apparatus jammed inside the well. Operations were stalled for nine days. Finishing off this "well from hell" would require particularly focused cost and scheduling skills. Though safety was given serious formal emphasis and was supported by an elaborate electronic sensor system, the production schedule was clearly dominant.

On this very day, indeed, BP VIPs had come prepared to commend the crew for its excellent safety record. Safety on this operation was heavily stressed in all of the formal ways. Before undertaking a task, crew members were routinely required to prepare in writing a list of all possible hazards that it would subject them to. The safety manual that ruled the operation received high praise from experts. Sensors for detection of fire and well gas were positioned throughout the vessel, sending instant input to consoles on the bridge, the drill shack and the engine control room. An emergency shutdown system on the bridge would instantly disable the most critical systems on board when activated.

Offsetting the extensive safety procedures and systems were an equally daunting system of incentives and limitations on action. Bonuses for the crew and executives overseeing the operation were based on meeting schedules. As delays were encountered, schedules were quickly, sometimes daily revised to pick up lost time, pressuring the crew to cut corners. The safety manual, however thorough, was ambiguous about when emergency action was to be taken, cautioning particularly against the tendency to overreaction. As originally designed, the sensor system would have automatically signaled evacuation of the rig when high levels of methane gas were detected. It had since been reset for manual activation, ostensibly out of concern that false alarms would needlessly disturb sleeping crew members. Training for activation of the system and how to respond to general crisis was lacking for key crew members.

Training, indeed, was lacking in many crucial respects. The sole emergency practice for the full crew was a life boat evacuation drill. Despite the obvious hazards inherent in this drilling operation there was no training for the worst case, the blowout that could overwhelm the Deep River Horizon's defenses and the fire that could follow. The drilling crew had a fixed procedure for response to any blow-out that got past the blowout preventer, five thousand feet down. Floor hands were expected to quickly install a special valve. Confronted with the real crisis on this day, there were no floor hands available. Now, the drilling crew had a choice. It could divert the gushing mud and gas out to sea, a measure that would require cleanup and an investigation, or it could funnel it to a mud-gas separator. If the separator was overwhelmed, more drastic action that would disable the rig would be required. In absolute worst case, drillers could activate hydraulic shears to seal off the flow from below, thereby disabling drilling capability altogether. In the absence of these stronger measures methane gas coursing up the umbilical from the seabed below could quickly over spread the rig threatening fire at the least hint of ignition. In the nine minutes from mud gushing out of the head until the ensuing explosion that day, drillers fought to gain control without executing any worst case measures.

The drilling crew that courageously labored to control this disaster did not survive to confirm the scenario that emerged. For those nine minutes following appearance of a fountain of gushing mud on the drilling deck, human judgment elsewhere on the ship was paralyzed. Glaring sensor lights on the bridge console that signaled deadly levels of methane throughout the rig brought no response. No alarm was sounded, engines were not shut down, no evacuation was ordered. Worst case was at hand, and it was overwhelmed by continued pursuit of cost and schedule priorities.

First notice of the crisis to most of those on board was eruption of explosion and fire. Only after that blast was the general alarm sounded. And, even though the rig was by then mortally damaged, burning and powerless, there was continued resistance on the bridge to cutting loose its connection to the sea floor. Disaster was so unthinkable that it was un-thought.[2]

The news story that followed was all about the horrendous oil spill that gushed forth on the sea floor from the failed blowout preventer. Oil soaked wildlife held forth on center stage in this monumental tragedy. Urgent investigation followed to identify the blameworthy or criminally responsible. The more plausible search was in the realm of management systems and methods. The Deep Water Horizon oil spill was caused by efficient pursuit of high priorities. Well paid, diligent, competent, well managed workers were failed by a management system focused firmly on priorities while it minimized or ignored worst case. Managers were intimidated by schedules and bonuses into paralysis of judgment.

Engineering is a technology, accounting is a technology, even operations priority setting is a technology, all practiced according to prevailing custom and rules. Management is often taught and practiced as if it were a decision making technology. It is not. Crisis response requires crisis decision making, not measured judgment. Risky decisions must be made. It is the manager's job to make them.

Not many Deep Water Horizon crisis decisions are called for in the course of a manager's career. Most day to day management crises involve breakdown of discipline or machinery. Management books rarely if at all teach management decision making at that level. They teach about empowering workers, building a climate of respect and integrity, promoting teamwork, growing talent. Like the myriad of management seminars regularly offered up as rites of passage into the new manager's role, they seek to inspire high ideals and noble objectives. The most consistent theme is likely to be how to succeed as boss by being a good person and implementing full scaled industrial democracy in the work place. Everything, it is assured, will work if the manager is only decisive and fair.

It is hard to argue with the tone and intent of prevailing management literature. It is also hard to take it seriously when faced on the job with passive resistance, workgroup collusion or worker rejection of rules and objectives, experiences faced by many managers. Behaviors like these are clear representation of badly deteriorated work attitudes. They happen because attempts at control have been inconsistent, poorly informed or excessive. They represent loss of commitment not just to high productivity, but to the vigor and success of the business. They arise out of poorly organized work processes and methods. They are fostered and reinforced by mediocre managing. At its worst, this is the work culture of "us and them", one that is most vulnerable to a union organizing campaign

Us and them is born from the perception of management as pervasively exploitive. Exploitation proceeds from harsh enforcement of tough or arbitrary rules that are intended to drive productivity up. Excessive control is mistaken for sound management. Solicitation of commitment is ignored or bypassed in favor of augmented worker apprehension and uncertainty. Cooperation is replaced with intimidation. Workers resist actively or passively. Management ratchets up the pressure. Productivity settles at a level established by the inevitable unspoken bargain of what constitutes a day's work for a day's pay. It is a stand-off. The culture descends into a pit of distrust and petty conflict. Once established, a culture of high control and contentiousness is fixed in place. It is a pattern I have seen play out through three major union strikes personally encountered through the course of my working career. The most recent of these, at the University of Bridgeport, almost ended my academic career.[3]

The best that can be attained out of a high-control culture is a solution like those achieved by Frederick Taylor and Henry

Ford. High production standards are set for workers. Active resistance to standards is met with disciplinary action. Workers are harassed or fired when they do not come into line. Specific performance standards are enforced. Taylor set and measured them in real time. Ford put workers in the assembly line straight jacket that commanded a full day's achievement of a machine driven standard. Enforced standards were supported in both cases by payment of premium wages. Workers who could not handle this bargain could quit. Those who could deal with it became part of America's emerging middle class.

The Taylor-Ford cultures succeeded because they were productive and essentially fair, though not always well received. The heavy hand of control generates blow-back. Those managers who fail to see beyond tight control and low wage structure as proper management policy will certainly end up with mediocre productivity and a fixed worker perception of managers as exploitative and uncaring. When the well of good will has been poisoned with acrimony, workers will likely organize to certify a labor union. That outcome will be a less than optimum solution for everyone. Once us and them has taken firm hold in the workplace, there are only two courses available. A compact of grudging mutual respect may emerge, or guerilla warfare between the controllers and controlled becomes the accepted way of work life. Guerilla war starts with a loss of mutual respect so profound that each party actively seeks opportunities to express its loathing of the other. In a marriage this ends with an ugly divorce. The business besieged by acrimonious strikes and work stoppages begins to shed labor in favor of automation and outsourcing. It is all free fall from there.

A culture of commitment built on respect, fairness and a realistic emphasis on productivity is the alternative. Commitment is a two-way street. Workers want commitment to a reasonable level of job security from their employers. Employers want worker commitment to the highest amount and quality of productivity that there is potential to achieve. Fundamental economic security is available only with competitive productivity, not just in product or service delivery but also in individual skill and capability. Businesses that settle into a comfortable groove end up in a rut. Managers and workers who accept their rut are destined to have their careers stuck in it.

Something like maximum productivity exists as a possibility for any ambitions, thoughtful manager to pursue. Most organizations operate somewhere between ten and thirty percent below potential. Reaching that potential is a worthwhile aspiration. Driving the system at maximum speed, though, has risk. If the road is bad, weather conditions poor, the vehicle poorly maintained, it can be a supremely foolish risk. BP was a well managed company in the sense of technology application, hiring, innovative work scheduling, pay, benefits and, within limits of the required risk, working conditions. It was a poorly managed company in terms of risk management. Incentives were too effective, caution against over-reaction too pervasive, focus on getting the job done too shallow.

Management is a craft that is practiced on a foundation of broad knowledge and applied with balanced judgment. Managers must do more than be good fellows. They must produce value through application of sound management practices. They must pursue good priorities while accounting for worst case and look for the best path to sustaining productivity. At the end of every day, week, month or year, there should be a clear sense of productive accomplishment.

There are no magic keys, no fixed answers, no fail-safe methods available to the working manager for achieving productivity. It begins with sound use of authority. Authority necessarily goes with the job though it is typically assigned under severe restraint and carries the risk of blow-back when used. Nonetheless it must be effectively used to establish necessary and reasonable boundaries of worker behavior. Within those boundaries, the extent of necessary worker freedom to exercise initiative must be astutely estimated, communicated and encouraged. Authority must not be allowed to become an impediment or barrier to productivity. Control cannot be permitted to become an end in itself. Workers must be embraced as individuals, not as members of a faceless class. Workers who have their individuality preserved and respected can offer commitment. Commitment is the foundation of high productivity.

Productivity is sustained through appeal to the uniqueness of each person. The disutility of job satisfaction as a lever on work motivation is a function of the variety of ways in which individuals find their satisfaction. Some sustain satisfaction despite disappointment, others refuse to be satisfied by anything less than the best outcome. Workers at either polarity of that range can be assets or liabilities depending on how they are managed.

In bringing forth the best productive effort of each worker, there are multiple variables in play that the manager must recognize. Level of pay, kind of pay plan, closeness or leniency of supervisory control, work challenge, opportunity for skill acquisition, relations with team members or co-workers, all figure in the motivational equation, and there is a unique equation for each individual. The high productivity manager solves that equation, person by person.

The craft of managing is not a single skill or method. It is a set of skills and methods adopted from a Chinese menu that can be re-mixed adaptively to fit differences in organization structure and worker temperament. The craft is in selecting the right mix to fit circumstances and putting the package together with competence. The right level and tactics of control, an understanding of how expectations are moderated to limit dissatisfaction, skilled application of problem solving intervention, sound practice of efficiency and capacity management techniques, application of astute judgment that balances priority and principle, these and more all go into the mix. It's complicated. But it is worth the effort.

Notes and References

1.   THE FOUNDATIONS OF CONTROL AND AUTHORITY

(1)   William Lanegwiesche, 2003. Unbuilding the World Trade Center. North Point Press.

2.   GOALS: MOTIVATION THEORY THAT WORKS

(1)   Maslow's Hierarchy of Needs, Wikipedia.com

(2)   Stephen Reiss, 2002, Who am I? The 16 Basic Desires That Motivate Our Actions and Define Our Personalities. Berkeley Trade.

(3)   Douglas Kenrick et al, May, 2010. Renovating the Pyramid of Needs, published in Perspectives on Psychological Science, 5,3.

(4)   David McClelland, 1961. The Achieving Society. The Free Press.

(5)   Frederick Herzberg, 1993. The Motivation to Work, Transaction Publishers.

(6)   Frederick W. Taylor, 1911. Scientific Management. New York Harper.

(7)   Peter Drucker, Wikipedia.com

(8)   Edwin A. Locke. 1976. The Nature and Causes of Job Satisfaction in Handbook of Industrial and Organizational Psychology, M. Dunnette, Ed.

(9)   Edwin Locke and Gary Latham, 1990. A Theory of Goal Setting and Task Performance, Prentice Hall.

(10) Edwin Locke and Gary Latham, 1984. Goal Setting: A Motivational Technique That Works, Prentice Hall.

(11) Edwin Locke et al, 1981. Goal Setting and Task Performance: 1969-1980. Psychological Bulletin, 90,1, pp 125-152.

(12) J. Stacy Adams, 1965. Inequity in social exchange. Adv. Exp. Soc. Psychol. 62:335-343.

3.   THE EXERCISE OF POWER AND AUTHORITY

(1)   www.hrworld.com/features/top-10-leadership-qualities-031908

(2)   Glenn Bassett, 1981. The Problem Employee Interview. AMACOM

4.   CONTRACTS AND GOVERNMENT REGULATION; UBER-
       CONTROL

(1)   Wikipedia.com, At-Will Employment.

(2)   Charles J. Muhl, January 2001. The Employment At-Will Doctrine:
       Three Major Exceptions. Monthly Labor Review. www.bls.gov/opub/
       mlr/2001/01/art1full.pdf

(3)   National Labor Relations Board, The National Labor Relations Act of
       1935 as Amended. www.nlrb.gov/about_us/overview/national_labor_
       relations_act.aspx

(4)   www.Wikipedia.com/wiki/National Labor Relations Act

5.   SCIENCE AND THE WORKER

(1)   Edwin A. Locke, 1976, The Nature and Causes of Job Satisfaction.
       In Handbook of Industrial and Organizational Psychology, Marvin D.
       Dunnette, editor

(2)   James K. Harter et al, July, 2010, Causal Impact of Employee Work
       Perceptions on the Bottom Line of Organizations. Perspectives in
       Psychological Science, American Psychological Society. L(Work
       Perceptions = Job Satisfaction).

(3)   Ryan Olson et al. January 2004. What We Teach Students about
       the Hawthorne Studies; A Review of Content within a Sample of
       Introductory I-O and OB Textbooks. The Industrial-Organizational
       Psychologist. Society for Industrial and Organizational Psychology.

(4)   www.referenceforbusiness.com/encyclopedia Hawthorne Experiments

(5)   www.wikipedia.com/phoebuscartel

(6)   Fritz J. Roethlisberger and William J. Dickson, 1939. Management
       and the Worker; An Account of the Research Program Conducted by
       the Western Electric Company, Hawthorne Works, Chicago. Harvard
       University Press.

(7)   Richard H. Franke and James D. Kaul, October 1978. The Hawthorne
       Experiments: First Statistical Interpretation. American Sociological
       Review, 43,5: 623-643.

(8)   Alex Cary, 1967. The Hawthorne Studies; A Radical Criticism. The
       American Sociological Review, 32; 403-416

(9)   Steven D. Levitt & John A. List, May 2009. Was There Really a
       Hawthorne Effect at the Hawthorne Plant? An Analysis of the Original

Illumination Experiments. Working Paper 15016, National Bureau Of Economic Research.

(10) Roethlisberger and Dickson, 1939, pages 189 through 376 of the published report.

6. THE JOB SATISFACTION CONUNDRUM

(1) www.wikipedia.com/wiki/meta-analysis

(2) Arthur H. Brayfield and Walter H. Crockett, 1955. Employee Attitudes and Employee Performance. Psychological Bulletin, 52:5, 396-424.

(3) Edwin A. Locke, 1976, The Nature and Causes of Job Satisfaction. In Handbook of Industrial and Organizational Psychology, Marvin D. Dunnette, editor.

(4) Richard L. Oliver, 2009. Satisfaction; A Behavioral Perspective On the Consumer, 2nd Edition. Published by M. E. Sharpe.

(5) Glenn A. Bassett, 1993. The Evolution and Future of High Performance Management Systems. Quorum Books.

7. PARTICIPATION, SATISFACTION & COMMITMENT - IT'S COMPLICATED

(1) Charles D. Wrege and Ronald G. Greenwood, 1991. Frederick W. Taylor; The Father of Scientific Management. Business One Irwin.

(2) Frederick W. Taylor, 1911. Scientific Management. Harper.

(3) www.wikipedia.com/wiki/employee engagement

(4) Barbara S. Romzek, 1989. Personal Consequences of Employee Commitment, Academy of Management Journal 32,3: 649-661.

(5) Lester Coch and John R.P. French, Jr. 1948. Overcoming Resistance to Change. Human Relations, 1: 512-532.

(6) James P. Curry et al, 1986. On the Causal Ordering of Job Satisfaction and Organizational Commitment. Academy of Management Journal, 29,4: 847-858

(7) Barbara Brown, 2003. Employees' Organizational Commitment and Their Perception of Supervisors' ,Relations-Oriented and Task-Oriented Leadership Behaviors, Virginia Polytechnic Institute Doctoral Dissertation. www.scholar.edu.lib.vt/theses

(8) www.wikipedia.com/wiki/quality circles.

(9)   John L. Cotton et al. 1988. Employee Participation: Diverse Forms and Different Outcomes, Academy of Management Review, 13,1: 8-22.

8.   HOW MUCH COMMITMENT GROWS ON THE MONEY TREE?

(1)   Edwin A. Locke et al, 1980. The Relative Effectiveness of Four Methods of Motivating Employee Performance, in K. D. Duncan, Editor, Changes in Working Life, John Wiley and Son.

(2)   Ben Hamper, 1991. Rivethead: Tales from the Assembly Line. Warner Books.

(3)   CIA/FOIA Reading Room, Document SOV-10020, 5/1/1989

(4)   Edwin A. Locke et al, 1980. The Relative Effectiveness of Four Methods of Motivating Employee Performance, in K. D. Duncan, Editor, Changes in Working Life, John Wiley and Son.

(5)   Harvard Business Review, Cambridge MA; Lincoln Electric Cases.

(6)   www.wikipedia.org/wiki/Profit Sharing

(7)   Mason Haire et al, August 1967. A Psychological Study of Pay. Journal of Applied Psychology Monograph, 51(4) Part 2 of 2, Whole # 636.

(8)   www.bls.gov/data/

9.   SOME NOTES ON THE POWER OF A CONVERSATION

(1)   www.wikipedia.org/wiki/Intelligence Quotient/Large Scale World War Testing.

(2)   www.wikipedia.org/wiki/SAT

(3)   Edwin E. Ghiselli, 1973, The Validity of Aptitude Tests in Personnel Selection. Personnel Psychology Journal, 26:461-477.

(4)   J. M. Digman, 1990. Personality structure: Emergence of the five-factor model. Annual Review of Psychology, 41, 417–440.

(5)   Murray R. Barrick, and Michael K. Mount , 1991 The Big-Five Personality Dimensions and Job Performance: A Meta-Analysis. Personnel Psychology Journal, 44:1

(6)   Frank L. Schmidt & John E. Hunter, 1992. Development of a Causal Model of Processes Determining Job Performance. Current Directions in Psychological Science. 1(3): 89-92.

(7)   Mitchell J. Neubert and Michael K. Mount, 1998. Relating Member Ability and Personality to Work-Team Processes and Team Effectiveness. Journal of Applied Psychology, 83:3, 377-391.

10. SPECIALIZATION, QUALITY OF WORK LIFE AND THE LEARNING CURVE

(1) can be downloaded online at http://www.econlib.org/library/Smith/smWN.html

(2) Thomas G. Cummings and E.S. Molloy, 1977. Improving Productivity and the Quality of Work Life. Praeger.

(3) http://www.en.wikipedia.org/wiki/learning_curves

(4) http://www.data.bls.gov/cgi-bin/surveymost?pr

(5) Herbert G Meyer, Emanuel Kay and John R.P. French Jr., 1965. Split Roles in Performance Appraisal, Harvard Business Review, 43(1): 123-129.

11. EFFICIENCY -- ENGINEERED TIME AND MOTION

(1) http://en.wikipedia.org/wiki/Energy_efficiency_conversion

(2) http://en.wikipedia.org/wiki/Efficiency_Movement

(3) http://en.wikipedia.org/wiki/Technocracy_movement

(4) Robert Lacey, 1986. FORD; The Men and the Machine, Little Brown.

(5) Frederick W. Taylor, 1911. Scientific Management, Harper.

(6) Charles D. Wrege & Ronald G. Greenwood, 1991. Frederick W. Taylor: The Father of Scientific Management - Myth and Reality. Business One Irwin.

(7) http://en.wikipedia.org/wiki/Motion_analysis

(8) Glenn Bassett, 1980. Part Time Work in Manufacturing, Consulting Report to General Electric Corporate Relations, Fairfield, Ct.

(9) Horace Middleton Vernon, 1921. Industrial Efficiency and Fatigue. Read at http://openlibrary.org/authors/Horace_Middleton Vernon

12. PRODUCTIVITY AND THE CAPACITY-COST CRUNCH

(1) Robert Lacey, 1986. FORD; The Men and the Machine, Little Brown.

(2) Loosely based on Eliyahu Goldratt's The Goal, 2004, North River Press

(3) Glenn A. Bassett, 1991. Management Strategies for Today's Project Shop Economy, Quorum Books.

13. BALANCED JUDGEMENT: RESULTS VS. RISK

(1) Nassim Taleb, 2007. The Black Swan: The Impact of Highly Improbable Events. Random House.

(2) David Barstow, David Rohde & Stephanie Saul, December 26, 2010, Deep River Horizon's Final Hours. New York Times.

(3) Glenn Bassett (2003). UB's Militant Union History: An Informed Participant and Labor Relations Specialist's Perspective. Journal of Academic Ethics 1 (3):287-294.

www.ingramcontent.com/pod-product-compliance
Lightning Source LLC
Chambersburg PA
CBHW051454170526
45166CB00001B/242